PHYSICIAN-ASSISTED SUICIDE

Other Books in the At Issue Series:

PHYSICIAN-ASSISTED SUICIDE

David Bender, *Publisher*
Bruno Leone, *Executive Editor*

Brenda Stalcup, *Managing Editor*
Scott Barbour, *Series Editor*

Daniel A. Leone, *Book Editor*

An Opposing Viewpoints® Series

Greenhaven Press, Inc.
San Diego, California

Library of Congress Cataloging-in-Publication Data

Physician-assisted suicide / Daniel A. Leone, book editor.
    p.   cm. — (At issue)
    Includes bibliographical references and index.
    ISBN 1-56510-019-0 (lib. : alk. paper). — ISBN 1-56510-018-2
(pbk. : alk. paper)
    1. Assisted suicide—Miscellaneous. I. Leone, Daniel A.,
1969– . II. Series: At issue (San Diego, Calif.)
R726.P492   1998
179.7—dc21   97-27792
                                                                    CIP

© 1998 by Greenhaven Press, Inc., PO Box 289009,
San Diego, CA 92198-9009

Printed in the U.S.A.

Table of Contents

Introduction

On June 26, 1997, the U.S. Supreme Court ruled that individuals do not have a fundamental, constitutional right to physician-assisted suicide. This ruling reversed two previous decisions by U.S. courts of appeals. In the first case, *Washington State vs. Glucksberg*, the Ninth Circuit court had determined that a Washington State law prohibiting individuals from aiding in suicides was unconstitutional. The court supported its decision by concluding that individuals have a constitutionally protected right under the Due Process Clause of the Fourteenth Amendment to control the timing and method of their death. In *New York vs. Quill*, in a ruling similar to the Ninth Circuit's decision, the Second Circuit court of appeals had declared unconstitutional a New York State law that prohibited assisting someone in committing suicide. The court justified its decision by arguing that the law violated the Equal Protection Clause of the Fourteenth Amendment. Both courts' decisions had, in effect, recognized a constitutional "right to die."

Although the Supreme Court overturned the decisions of the two courts of appeals, its ruling did not put an end to the debate over assisted suicide. As Justice Sandra Day O'Connor noted, the Court concluded that there "is no generalized right to commit suicide." However, the Court emphasized that its decision and the Constitution do not place absolute restrictions on state law, leaving open the possibility for states to create their own laws to establish such a right. In addition, the Court indicated that laws that prohibit physician-assisted suicide could still be challenged in specific cases in the future. According to legal experts who evaluated the decision, the Court recognized that physician-assisted suicide is a complicated issue and that each case has a unique set of circumstances that must be evaluated separately. In short, the Court shifted the responsibility for this issue to the states, and by doing so it indirectly ensured that the controversy and legal battles over physician-assisted suicide will continue.

What is physician-assisted suicide?

There are varying degrees to which a person can be involved in hastening the death of a terminally ill individual. It is important to understand the terms for and distinctions between these degrees. Euthanasia, a word that is often associated with physician-assisted suicide, is defined by the *Merriam-Webster Dictionary* as "the act or practice of killing for reasons of mercy." There are two types of euthanasia: passive and active. Passive euthanasia takes place when life-saving measures are withheld or withdrawn and the terminally ill person is allowed to die of natural causes. A son's electing to take his mother off life-support machines, which leads to her death, would be an example of passive euthanasia. Today, there is little controversy and debate over passive euthanasia. The constitutional right of a patient (or if the patient is incompetent, the patient's guardian) to refuse treatment was established in 1976 by the Supreme Court's decision in the case of Karen Ann Quinlan. In 1975, Quinlan fell into an irreversible coma after a drug overdose and was put on a life-support system. Her parents, who wished to bring an end to their family's suffering, met resistance after requesting that their daughter be removed from life support. They fought a legal battle all the way to the Supreme Court. The Court decided in favor of Quinlan's parents and granted them the right to remove their daughter from the system, establishing a legal precedent for passive euthanasia.

In active euthanasia, a person actually causes the death of a terminally ill individual. For example, a person who gives a dying friend a lethal injection to hasten death would be performing active euthanasia. Although active euthanasia is presently illegal, many medical professionals claim that it is practiced in secrecy on a regular basis. Active euthanasia is highly controversial: Its critics argue that patients are often not informed of what is being done to them or are coerced into agreeing to the act.

Assisted suicide takes place when a dying person who wishes to precipitate death requests help in carrying out the act. There is a distinction between assisted suicide and euthanasia. In euthanasia, the dying patients may or may not be aware of what is happening to them and may or may not have requested to die. In an assisted suicide, the terminally ill person wants to die and has specifically asked for help. Physician-assisted suicide occurs when the individual assisting in the suicide is a doctor rather than a friend or family member. Because doctors are the people most familiar with their patients' medical condition and have knowledge of and access to the necessary means to cause certain death, terminally ill patients who have made the decision to end their lives often turn to their physicians for advice and help. Studies indicate, however, that many physicians are unwilling to provide their assistance in suicide because it conflicts with their ethical beliefs or because it is illegal.

The controversy over legalization

Much of the controversy surrounding euthanasia focuses on the debate over whether physician-assisted suicide should be legalized. Supporters of legalization believe that terminally ill individuals have the right to end their own lives in some instances. Because physician-assisted suicide is illegal, they maintain, many patients are unable to get the help necessary to end their lives and must involuntarily endure extreme pain and suffering. Others argue that physician-assisted suicide must be legalized for purposes of regulation. They contend that in spite of current law, the practice is conducted regularly in secrecy; therefore, the potential for abuse already exists. According to Cheryl Smith, former staff attorney for the Hemlock Society, "Legalization, with medical record documentation and reporting requirements, will enable authorities to regulate the practice and guard against abuses, while punishing the real offenders."

On the other hand, opponents of physician-assisted suicide argue that legalization would cause abuse rather than reduce or control it. They maintain that legalized assisted suicide would lead to the deaths of patients who do not really wish to die. For example, they contend that influential doctors or family members, unrestricted by law, may persuade patients to choose death or that greedy insurance companies may pressure doctors to control insurance costs by ending lives prematurely.

Others worry that legalized assisted suicide would be the first step down the "slippery slope" that would lead to widespread, unregulated mercy killing of individuals whom society considers undesirable or whose lives have been arbitrarily deemed not worth living. As expressed by legal experts Robert George and William Porth, "It is not unrealistic to fear that government may assume what began as a private prerogative, and move from making life-and-death decisions for the comatose, to making them for the insane, for the retarded, for those of less than average intelligence, and finally for those who are entirely rational and intelligent, but whose desire to cling to life brands them as obstinate, uncooperative, and just plain unreasonable." These fears lead many to oppose physician-assisted suicide even under carefully regulated conditions.

The legalization of physician-assisted suicide is an extremely sensitive, complicated, and controversial topic. If future legislation is to be successful, it will need to protect both the rights of terminally ill patients who rationally choose death and the rights of weak or incompetent patients who do not wish to die. This anthology, *At Issue: Physician-Assisted Suicide*, explores a variety of perspectives on the legal, ethical, and moral aspects of physician-assisted suicide.

1

Physicians Should Assist in Suicide

Jack Kevorkian, interviewed by John A. Pridonoff

Jack Kevorkian is a retired pathologist and a prominent advocate of physician-assisted suicide. He was interviewed by John A. Pridonoff, the executive director of Timelines, *the official newsletter of the Hemlock Society.*

Patients should not hesitate to ask their physicians for aid-in-dying. Unfortunately, because physician-assisted suicide is illegal, most patients are afraid to request it and doctors are reluctant to discuss the option. However, a doctor's duty, in addition to preserving life and health, is to minimize pain and suffering. Therefore, under the appropriate circumstances, doctors should be allowed to assist patients in dying.

John A. Pridonoff: As a physician you have insight into the psychology of your profession. How would you recommend patients approach their physicians on the issue of aid-in-dying?

Jack Kevorkian: If the circumstances were correct and favorable, the patient should have no qualms about approaching the issue directly. Any question or comment that the patient makes or wants to make should be accepted by the doctor with equanimity and answered honestly. It's as simple as that.

Is that the way you see the medical situation today?

No. Doctors are afraid. Patients are afraid. Everyone's afraid to take any step. And, when it's taken, it's taken on eggshells. Doctors are afraid that any patient at any time may say, "Doctor, I've had enough." The doctor will then say, "Well, let's see if you've had enough. Wait a minute! We've got some treatment we haven't tried yet, so we're going to do it, but when the time comes, don't worry, we'll help you. We want the best, the most life you can possibly have. You've got to trust us on that." And when doctors do and say things like that, the patients trust them, lose their fear, and go along with recommendations that they would otherwise refuse.

From "The Dialogue Begins: An interview with Dr. Jack Kevorkian," interview by John A. Pridonoff, *Timelines*, March/April 1994. Reprinted by permission of the Hemlock Society.

Often patients will have an on-going relationship with their personal physicians. However, when they are diagnosed with cancer, they are sent to an oncologist.

That's right.

With this unfamiliar doctor, how can patients find out how the doctor feels about giving them aid-in-dying, if it comes to that?

The same way as I said before. If the patient's doctor dodges it because of some personal qualm, opinion, or religious basis, then the patient should always work through a nurse. The patient *should* have access to such a doctor, such counsel, at any time, because the service should be available always.

Let's operate on the premise that physician aid-in-dying is against the law, as it is now.

Well, that's different. Under the present conditions I don't know how they should approach it, because every case is different. No matter how the doctor feels, she's going to be defensive. She's going to have the fear that you're treading into an area that she fears entirely, and fear that you're approaching something she knows nothing about. She also has the fear of censure by her colleagues. It's this mixture that's going to force her to be very reticent and evasive. So it's very difficult, and many patients don't even open the subject. They don't want to offend or antagonize the doctor and maybe influence negatively their current treatment program. They know that the chance of getting cooperation is almost nil.

What do you feel should be different? What is the basic responsibility of a physician?

Simple, what every real oath says. A physician is supposed to help patients maintain or regain health and avoid suffering. He's got to juggle this as he goes along; that's why it's an art of medicine, not a science.

A physician is supposed to help patients maintain or regain health and avoid suffering.

With appropriate safeguards, do you believe that voluntary physician aid-in-dying for terminally ill people can be seen as a redeeming act?

Certainly, just as any medical service can be seen as a redeeming act. If this taboo is such a profound intimidation that you need a special law to allow it, then OK, treat it like any *medical service.* When a patient wants something, the doctor has to find out if he needs it. Some doctors don't care about that, they satisfy the want. We call them charlatans, quacks, out to make money. The *patient* has the *want.* The *doctor* has to legitimize it as a *need.* And then the patient has a claim on the doctor, on the physician's services. See? *The claim becomes a patient's right under those circumstances. So* then the doctor says, "Is the want justified? Yes, the want is justified." The want *then* becomes a need. Then it's up to the doctor to say, "At what point is my intervention required?" Now he uses his *expertise,* his *training* and his *experience* to determine if the patient's want is a real, justifiable need. It's really basically simple, but when you expound on it philosophically, it sounds complicated.

What is the central aim of the MERCY Amendment and what do the letters [MERCY] stand for?

The letters MERCY stand for Movement Ensuring the Right to Choose for Yourself. And the aim is not only central, but sole—to reiterate, to make explicit and objectify [this right] as best we can. You can't objectify an abstraction. Only a language can do that. We objectify the right, the right that has always existed, but was never honored.

And you're saying that right is what?

The right to choose not to suffer. Not to suffer unduly when it's not necessary and cannot be remunerated.

And all that would be fleshed out by the legislature or the medical society?

Yes, by the rulers, by the guidelines set down for it. For example, we have a right to assembly, do we not? In the Bill of Rights? That right has always existed in a free society, but unfortunately had to be objectified because of our corrupt society. But does any law tell you *how* to assemble? You have guidelines for assemblies. Written and unwritten. Right? We also have freedom of the press. Does anyone tell the press *how* to operate? The law? Only within certain strict guidelines, which already exist for medicine. The medical service will be done competently and honestly or the doctor will be prosecuted. The laws exist! So you lay down the guidelines once the right is established—once the right has been *acknowledged*. That's the word.

Tens of thousands of our [Hemlock Society] national membership are supporters of you and your medical practice. Thousands sent postcards to the Governor's Commission on Death and Dying urging the repeal of the anti-assisted suicide law. They are committed to the end of pain and suffering of terminally ill people. What would you like to say to them?

Well, first I thank members of The Hemlock Society U.S.A. for taking the time and effort to send the cards and letters. I appreciate what they did. It shows a high degree of commitment on their part. Now, we have a chance to see how committed everyone else is.

Is there anything you would like to say, that I didn't cover in the questions?

No, those are fair questions. I'm glad I can get a working relationship going with Hemlock, which, unfortunately, I couldn't do with the prior executive director. I think, it's not a matter anymore of anyone striving for leadership, glory or distinction. Now the aim is to get this right affirmed, so that patients can get the help they need from doctors who want to give it, without intimidation or fear.

Several right-to-die organizations have formed over the past several years. As we try to deal with the complex issues that have developed, bottom line, who's most important?

The patient.

2
Physicians Should Not Assist in Suicide

Anneke Quinta

Anneke Quinta is a resident in family practice at Kingston Hospital in New York.

Growing public support for physician-assisted suicide is a dangerous trend. The rationale that led to the systematic death programs of the Holocaust can be traced to a proposal from Hitler's German Justice Ministry asking for the legalization of physician-assisted suicide as a means to end suffering for incurable patients. No one should be allowed to assist in the taking of life. Physicians must respect the sanctity of life and focus on providing care and comfort to the terminally ill so that dying will be a less unpleasant experience.

"Help me to die," she said. I looked down at Margaret in surprise. The witty Welsh woman had been my patient for several weeks. A veteran of our surgical unit, she had weathered several major operations and now faced another. Usually optimistic, she shared my opinion that this hospital stay would be her last.

Margaret's request seemed reasonable. Her mind was clear. She understood her deteriorating condition and concluded that the best thing I could do for her was to end her life. She had a terminal illness and wanted to spare herself and her family the pain of prolonged suffering. She was competent to make a decision and clearly stated her wish.

Over the ensuing weeks, Margaret's pain grew worse. One by one, conventional methods of pain relief failed, and my feelings of inadequacy increased. Margaret often asked me to help her die. Faced with her request, I could no longer skirt the issue. Should doctors help patients like her commit suicide? Many consider physician-assisted suicide the ultimate in personal choice. With a few guidelines, they believe, Margaret and others like her could have their wish. A recent University of Michigan study offers three guidelines. First, the patient must be a mentally competent adult whose death is expected within six months. Second, the

From Anneke Quinta, "The Assisted Suicide Debate," *Plough*, no. 52, Summer 1997. Reprinted by permission of the *Plough*.

patient must request her physician's assistance to end her life on more than one occasion. Third, a second physician must examine the patient and agree with the diagnosis and outlook. The study found that 66 percent of the public and 56 percent of the physicians surveyed favored the legalization of physician-assisted suicide if such guidelines were used.[1]

Do we know what we are choosing? Perhaps we can learn from the Netherlands, a nation where similar guidelines are already in effect. To determine how well the system was working, the Dutch government collected data on 8,100 cases in which doctors prescribed lethal overdoses of medication. They found that 61 percent of the patients had not consented to their death.[2] Doctors defended their actions by saying they did what they believed the patient or the patient's family wanted. However, in 45 percent of these cases, doctors didn't even consult family members.[3]

Two recent legal cases further show that abuse occurs despite regulations. In one, a psychiatrist helped a depressed but physically healthy patient commit suicide without treating the depression. The court merely reprimanded the doctor, saying his action undermined faith in the medical profession. In another case, a gynecologist gave a fatal injection to a severely handicapped baby. The appeals court ruled that the doctor made a "justified choice."

Physician-assisted suicide and the Holocaust

Why have the Dutch fallen so disastrously short of complying with their own guidelines, despite the "advanced" environment provided by their modern healthcare and legal systems? Are they an exception or the rule? Consider this excerpt from a *New York Times* article:

> The memorandum . . . proposed that "it shall be made possible for physicians to end the tortures of incurable patients, upon request, in the interests of true humanity." Incurability would be determined not only by the attending physician, but also by two official doctors who would carefully trace the history of the case and personally examine the patient . . . the patient himself shall "expressly and earnestly" ask it, or "in case the patient no longer is able to express his desire, his nearer relatives, acting from motives that do not contravene morals, shall so request."[4]

This rhetoric sounds like something from the current debate on physician-assisted suicide, and the guidelines it proposes are similar to those favored by a majority of today's physicians and the public. Yet the article is from 1933, and the memorandum it quotes was issued by none other than Hitler's German Justice Ministry.

In one [recent legal case], a psychiatrist helped a depressed but physically healthy patient commit suicide.

The outcome of this memorandum warrants further examination. The German Medical Association set up a system to implement the proposal, legalizing physician-assisted suicide. Doctors started on competent patients with terminal illnesses who requested it, then mentally incompetent patients, and eventually anyone economically—or ideologically— unprofitable to the state. Between 1933 and 1941, over seventy thousand "futile or terminal" patients were killed *in German hospitals.*

The "right" to die could become a death sentence for the most vulnerable.

To the State, the main benefit of the "T4 Euthanasia Program," as it came to be known, was economic. It saved 88 million Reichmarks per year.[5] The program was "geared toward economic performance in the healthcare market and cost efficient utilization of limited resources."[6] (Sound like a contemporary medical economics journal?) To increase efficiency, the Nazis moved the technology developed in the T4 killing hospitals to specialized centers—death camps.

For many in our society today, the premise that certain human lives are not worth saving is not a shocking one. It may be a well-guarded one, hidden by euphemisms and denied under fire; nonetheless, it underlies widespread approval of physician-assisted suicide, and this is why the historical lesson applies to our situation. . . . Call me an alarmist, but as far as I can see, a dangerously similar combination of the factors in play in Germany during the 1930s influences American healthcare today.

Public opinion favors physician-assisted suicide, and court rulings mirror this. The Ninth Circuit Court of Appeals recently overturned Washington State's ban on physician-assisted suicide, saying the "right to determine the time and manner of one's death" outweighed the state's duty to preserve life.[7] "Quality of life" has replaced the time-honored concept of "sanctity of life."

Powerful managed care companies, obsessed with efficient resource utilization, now control much of healthcare. Increasingly, cost seems to influence the care of the dying more than anything else. Without quality medical care available and affordable for all, the poor may soon be forced to "choose" suicide instead of costly extended care. It is easy to see how the "right" to die could become a death sentence for the most vulnerable.

So what of Margaret? It is clear to me that given its track record—historical and contemporary—we can never allow physician-assisted suicide in our country. It is also clear to me, as a Christian, that no one has a right to assist another in taking her own life or in deciding the hour of death. All the more, we must meet the challenge of making dying as positive and comfortable an experience as possible.

As doctors, nurses, and care providers, we must provide more than healthcare, and as families we must provide more than money. But we must also do more, and we can start on a very simple, personal level. We must make our patients, our relatives, our elderly neighbors, and our colleagues feel so wanted and needed that they will not want to die. Instead of shunning the dying or making them feel (however subtly) that they are a burden on us, we must surround them with love. When this happens, will assisted suicide still be an issue?

Notes

1. J.G. Bachman et. al, "Attitudes of Michigan Physicians and Public toward Legalizing Physician Assisted Suicide." *NEJM* 1996; 334:303–09.

2. *Medical Decisions about the End of Life* (transl. from the Dutch). The Hague, Netherlands: SDU, 1991.

3. *U.S. News & World Report,* April 25, 1994, 36.

4. *New York Times,* Oct. 8, 1933.

5. *Medizin im Nationalsozialismus: Ein Arbeitsbuch.* Tübingen, Germany: Schwäbische Verlagsgesellschaft, 1980, 25.

6. Hartmut M. Hanauske-Abel, "Not a Slippery Slope or Sudden Subversion: German Medicine and National Socialism in 1933." *BMJ* 1996; 313: 1453–63.

7. George J. Annas, "The Promised End: Constitutional Aspects of Physician-Assisted Suicide." *NEJM* 1996; 335:683–87.

3

Physician-Assisted Suicide Is Moral

Timothy E. Quill

*Timothy E. Quill is a doctor who helped a terminally ill patient, "Diane,"
commit suicide and then wrote about the experience in 1991 in the* New
England Journal of Medicine. *He is associate professor of medicine and
psychiatry and head of the program for biopsychosocial studies at the
University of Rochester School of Medicine and Dentistry in New York.*

Under certain circumstances, physician-assisted suicide can be
both morally and ethically acceptable. If a physically healthy but
severely depressed person seeks assistance in committing suicide,
the physician should not assist but should instead do everything
possible to treat the depression and prevent the suicide. However,
if a competent, terminally ill patient is suffering from tremendous
physical pain and requests that a physician aid in his or her death,
that physician is morally obligated to honor the patient's request.

The debate about physician-assisted death thus far has been clouded by
imprecise, sometimes inflammatory use of language. The descriptive
term "physician-assisted death" includes both physician-assisted suicide
and voluntary active euthanasia. It emphasizes the physician's role as an
assistant to an act initiated by the patient. Doctors "killing" patients is
technically correct, but it incorrectly suggests a physician-driven act, and
brings out uneasy visions of the Holocaust, in which a vicious abuse of
physician power was used to systematically exterminate those who were
deemed to be socially unworthy. Nothing could be further from the intent
of those who favor a limited reconsideration of public policy in the areas
of assisted suicide and voluntary active euthanasia. Physicians are reluctant
partners in assisted dying, motivated by the compassion they feel toward
suffering patients who request their help and have no good alternatives.

The different kinds of suicide

Suicide is defined as the intentional taking of one's own life, but its mul-
tilayered meaning emerges in a second definition which includes the self-

From *Death and Dignity: Making Choices and Taking Charge* by Timothy E. Quill, M.D. Copyright
©1994 by Timothy E. Quill. Reprinted by permission of W.W. Norton & Company, Inc.

destruction of one's own personal interests. In the medical literature, suicide is almost always viewed as an act of despair and self-destructiveness, the outgrowth of untreated depression and impaired rational thought. Suicide in that context is clearly something to be prevented, and physicians' appropriate role is to use all their resources, including enforced hospitalization if necessary, to help patients regain their will to live.

Suicide in the context of end-stage medical illness associated with irreversible suffering that can only end in death can have a different meaning. Many believe that suicide under such circumstances can be rational—it is hard to judge the wish for an end to intolerable suffering that can only end in death as irrational. Under such tragic circumstances, death can sometimes provide the only relief. The only question is, how much more one must endure until it comes. Yet, because patients with such severe medical conditions are usually sad if not clinically depressed, it can at times be difficult to determine whether emotional responses to their illnesses are distorting their decision making. If there is any question that depression or other mental illness is coloring the patient's judgment, then consultation by an experienced psychiatrist or psychologist is necessary to understand the full implications of an incurably ill patient's request for assisted death.

In "assisted suicide," a patient is still carrying out his own act.

In "assisted suicide," a patient is still carrying out his own act, but he is indirectly helped by an "assistant." When the assistant is motivated by compassion for an incurably ill patient who clearly and repeatedly requests help, the act can be ethical and moral, if not legal. If the assistant is motivated by greed, or if there is uncertainty about the rationality or motivation behind the patient's request, then the act of assistance becomes immoral, unethical, as well as illegal. There is little case-based legal definition for what kind of compassionate "assistance" might be considered illegal. For example, a physician might prescribe a potentially lethal supply of medication, along with information about what dose would be lethal and what dose would be medicinal. There the physician's intention could be explicitly to give the patient the option of taking her own life; or it might be more ambiguous. ("Don't take all of them or it could kill you.") Do we want dying patients to have such information and choice, or should we perhaps protect them from themselves by depriving them of potent medication that might be used to take their own lives? It is very difficult to prosecute doctors successfully in the face of such ambiguity, especially if they are clearly motivated by compassion for their terminally ill patients rather than self-interest.

Many dying patients often have potentially lethal doses of medication at home that are being used to treat their symptoms. To withhold such medicine because of an abstract fear about suicide would be immoral, and in violation of fundamental principles of comfort care. Unfortunately, some physicians continue to undermedicate potentially treatable symptoms of dying patients, in part out of vague fears about patient suicide, but probably as significantly by their fear of legal or professional investigation should their patient take an overdose. If the patient is suffering from a reversible depression that is distorting her judgment, then caution and conservatism must be exercised until the distortion is resolved. Yet undertreating a dying patient's symptoms because of unsubstantiated fears about liability is unfortunately quite legal, though clearly unethical and immoral.

Assisted suicide and the law

There are laws in thirty-six states, including New York State where I practice, prohibiting assisted suicide. The intent of these laws is presumably to prohibit persons from promoting a suicide for malicious intent, for example, by giving a loaded gun to a rich relative who is experiencing transient depression. No physician or family member has ever been convicted of assisting in the suicide of a severely ill patient with intractable suffering. Such acts appear to be looked upon by juries as acts of compassion not intended to be covered by the law. Yet the laws exist, and the threat of professional or legal repercussions is severe enough to prohibit many doctors from assisting their patients even when they consider the patients' requests rational and compelling. These laws perpetuate and exaggerate the power differences between vulnerable patients and their physicians, and put patients' fates more than ever at the discretion of their physicians.

In physician-assisted suicide, the patient commits the final act herself. The physician's participation is indirect, and there can always be a reasonable doubt about the intention as long as the prescribed drug has other medicinal uses. My patient, Diane, felt she had to be alone at her death in order to maintain this legal ambiguity, and to protect her family and me should her act ever be discovered. No one should *have* to be alone at death to protect anyone. Ironically and tragically, my innocence in the eyes of the grand jury, which investigated my involvement with Diane in response to the article [in the March 7, 1991, *New England Journal of Medicine*], was determined in no small measure by the fact that I was not present at her death. Laws that indirectly promote loneliness and abandonment at death should be carefully reconsidered to ensure that they don't have the unintended effect of further isolating and disempowering rather than protecting the dying person.

Laws that indirectly promote loneliness and abandonment at death should be carefully reconsidered.

Euthanasia is defined as the act of painlessly putting to death a person who is suffering from an incurable, painful disease or condition. Its definition suggests a quiet and easy death—a "good death." Euthanasia is equated by some with "mercy killing," and its mention raises worries about involuntary killing and progressive disregard for human life. For others, the images of a painless escape from extreme suffering into death offer the promise of more compassionate and humane options for the dying. Unlike assisted suicide, where the legal implications have yet to be fully clarified, euthanasia is illegal in all states in the United States and likely to be vigorously prosecuted. It is also illegal in all other countries, though in the Netherlands it is explicitly left unprosecuted provided that specific guidelines are met.

"Voluntary" and "involuntary" euthanasia

Several distinctions are of critical importance in a serious discussion about euthanasia. The first is "voluntary" versus "involuntary," and the second is "active" versus "passive." "Voluntary" euthanasia means that the act of putting the person to death is the end result of the person's own free will. Consideration of voluntary euthanasia as an option, and the request for its use, must emanate from the patient *and no one else.* The patient's rational thought processes must not be distorted by depression or other sources of cognitive impairment. Unlike assisted suicide, where the physician provides the means for the patient to subsequently use, in euthanasia the physician is the direct agent of death. Although voluntary euthanasia can potentially be as humane and morally justifiable as assisted suicide, it puts the physician in a very powerful position. Many physicians and policy makers feel great trepidation because of the potential for abuse (e.g., physician-initiated euthanasia on incompetent patients or in ambiguous situations) or error (e.g., the patient changing her mind at the last minute).

Voluntary euthanasia is an area worthy of our serious consideration.

"Involuntary" euthanasia means that the person is put to death without out explicitly requesting it. Although this could be an act motivated by compassion for a severely suffering, incompetent patient, there is too much subjectivity and personal variation in the definition of "suffering" to condone such "acts of mercy." Involuntary euthanasia could also be used for completely immoral purposes—for example, on incompetent or even competent persons as an act of eugenics and social manipulation. Such abuses were witnessed in Nazi Germany, as we should never forget. Involuntary euthanasia, even when compassionately motivated, should remain criminal, and should be vigorously prosecuted and prohibited.

Involuntary euthanasia is a fundamentally different act both morally and ethically from responding to a voluntary request for euthanasia by a competent patient who has no escape from his suffering other than death. Voluntary euthanasia is an area worthy of our serious consideration, since it would allow patients who have exhausted all other reasonable options to choose death rather than continue suffering. Involuntary euthanasia, even when compassionately motivated, is extremely dangerous ground because of the inevitable subjectivity and personal variation of human suffering, and because of the potential for social abuse when one starts making such profound decisions on behalf of other persons who cannot express their own wishes. Perhaps fully competent suffering persons should be given the possibility of making such decisions for themselves; but under no circumstances should we allow such decisions to be made on behalf of those who are incompetent.

"Active" and "passive" euthanasia

The distinction between "active" and "passive" euthanasia rests upon the assumption that it is ethically permissible for physicians to withhold or withdraw life-sustaining medical treatment at the patient's request, and let the patient die passively of "natural causes." Such "passive" euthanasia is based on the fundamental ethical principle that informed, autonomous patients have the right to refuse any and all medical treatments, no matter what the consequences. Yet, under circumstances of identical or even greater suffering where no life-sustaining treatment is being used, current law forbids the physician to take direct action designed to achieve the same end—even if it is rationally requested by the patient and would result in a more humane death. Passive euthanasia, along with the double effect of narcotic pain medicine, probably accounts for the vast majority of the estimated six thousand planned deaths in United States hospitals each day. How many times lines are secretly crossed and distinctions blurred in the care of these dying patients is simply not known.

An important distinction

Some ethicists believe that there is a fundamentally important distinction between active and passive euthanasia. Death is the intended outcome in both circumstances, but the physicians' actions are directly causal in active euthanasia, whereas it is the physicians' "inaction" in passive euthanasia that allows the patient to die of "natural causes." By maintaining this distinction, the medical profession allegedly remains untainted by becoming an agent of death. Yet, in the cloudy world of patient care, these distinctions can become more illusory than real, and our attempts to remain ethically pure sometimes extract a considerable price from dying persons who have little left to give. The intent of both active and passive euthanasia is to finally allow the patient with no other good options to die in the most humane way possible.

> *The intent of both active and passive euthanasia is to finally allow the patient with no other good options to die in the most humane way possible.*

One does not need to have a great deal of medical experience to find an example of passive euthanasia resulting in a very difficult death from "natural causes." Take for example a patient with end-stage, metastatic lung cancer who is near death from respiratory failure. He has tried to prolong his life through chemotherapy and radiation, but is now losing weight, extremely short of breath, and nearing the end of the road. He has elected to forgo cardiopulmonary resuscitation and mechanical ventilation (breathing machine) and knows that his death is inevitable. In fact, he has even begun to look forward to death as an escape from his life, which now feels completely empty, devoid of future or hope. So far, most physicians and ethicists would be comfortable with this example of passive euthanasia, allowing the person to die "naturally" of respiratory failure rather than prolonging his death by putting him on a mechanical ventilator.

Yet suppose that this patient has an overwhelming fear of suffocation, and wants to go to sleep quickly and not wake up, rather than continuing the agony of gradual suffocation for days or even weeks prior to his inevitable death. His request is confirmed to be rational, and his family agrees that he should be spared this final struggle if at all possible. Since there is no life-sustaining treatment to discontinue, passive euthanasia does not provide help or guidance at this point. According to comfort care principles, his shortness of breath can be treated with narcotics in doses intended to limit the feelings of discomfort, but not to intentionally produce death. His shortness of breath and feelings of extreme anxiety are therefore treated with an infusion of morphine until he falls asleep and appears relaxed. Yet periodically he awakens, thrashing and screaming from a terrifying feeling of suffocation. His morphine dose is appropriately increased to the point that he is relaxed enough to again lose consciousness, and no further. Unfortunately, a primitive drive to continue breathing sustains him whenever he drifts off into sleep. He alternates between periods of extreme agitation and a medicated sleep on the edge of death, where he lingers for over a week on gradually increasing doses of morphine before finally succumbing. Anyone who has witnessed such "natural deaths" cannot help but be troubled by their nightmarish quality.

An escape from suffering

The option of a physician-assisted death, whether by assisted suicide or active voluntary euthanasia, would allow patients such as this an escape from meaningless torment prior to death. When death is the only way to relieve suffering, and inevitable regardless, why not allow it to come in the most humane and dignified way possible? Why is it considered ethical to die of "natural causes" after a long heroic fight against illness filled with "unnatural" life-prolonging medical interventions, and unethical to allow patients to take charge at the end of a long illness and choose to die painlessly and quickly? Most of us hope to be fortunate enough to experience a "good death" when we have to die, and to be spared an agonizing ordeal at the very end. Many of us hope that if we do end up in such unfortunate circumstances, we can find a physician who will help us creatively explore all possibilities, including facilitating a relatively quick and painless death. Hopefully we will never need it, but the possibility would be very reassuring.

4

Physician-Assisted Suicide Is a Moral Dilemma

David A. Bennahum

David A. Bennahum is a professor of medicine and family and community medicine at the Center for Ethics, Law and the Humanities at the University of New Mexico, Albuquerque.

There are strong arguments both for and against physician-assisted suicide. It is a doctor's duty to relieve a patient's suffering and pain. However, sometimes the only relief available is death. Physicians face a moral dilemma in choosing between the duty to preserve life and the equally important responsibility to ease suffering.

I never saw a dead body until my first anatomy class. Today those who have willed their bodies to science receive letters of gratitude, visit with our students, and have their names put up on memorial plaques; but 37 years ago our subjects were derelicts and anonymous old men found dead in flop house hotels. George C., his name written on a tag tied to one toe, lay stretched out on one of the six dissecting tables in the anatomy laboratory that autumn morning when I was 22 and beginning medical school. I remember hesitating at the door and then joining my four partners at Mr. C.'s side, trepidation giving way to curiosity, the moment imprinted forever in my memory by the smell of formalin.

In the years of study and training that followed, I saw many people die. I participated in and led resuscitation efforts and rode the ambulance as a New York City intern. But experiences were often screened from memory by the intense routines of the day, the long nights and the permanent exhaustion of hospital training. Then one night a black toddler, living with his mother and brothers and sisters in a welfare hotel, was brought in unconscious after swallowing lighter fluid. Despite an intense hour of attempted resuscitation, we could not revive him; and finally, at a nurse's urging, I realized that we had failed and that I had to order the team to stop their efforts. Crossing the hall into the small room where the child's mother was waiting, I told her that her child had died. She never looked at me and I did not know how to reach her, did not know how to

From David A. Bennahum, "Encounters with Death," *Cambridge Quarterly of Healthcare Ethics*, vol. 5, no. 1, Winter 1996. Copyright ©1996 by Cambridge University Press. Reprinted by permission of Cambridge University Press.

penetrate the cloud of her despair. To this day I see his small body on the emergency room gurney. Had I failed? Could I have saved his life?

Acknowledging death's dominion did not come easily. It still surprises me how many years and how many patients it has taken for me to be ready for that part of my education. I had to experience my father's death to admit my own mortality. I suspect, like many physicians, I had gone from a prolonged adolescence directly into medicine; and, despite years of experience, I had remained, on a certain level, immature, invulnerable, and immortal, cloaked in the magical white coat of medicine. Returning with my wife and children from a year in Jerusalem, I was met at Orly airport and was told that my father was in a hospital in Paris suddenly ill with an intestinal obstruction. Surgery revealed pancreatic cancer, and a few months later I found myself standing beside my brother as we stumbled, in tears, through the Kaddish, the prayer for the dead, at his grave. But what did I learn from his death? Above all I learned to tell the patient the truth, for my mother, in her desire to protect, had been afraid to allow my father to be told that he had cancer. Of course he came to know; but we were forbidden by her proscription to talk about it, and so we denied him and each other a time of support, understanding, and resolution.

Doubting Death With Dignity

Although my first encounters were essential to my development as a physician, it was only from 1976 that my experience would be coupled with ethical analysis. At that time I joined a newly formed Death With Dignity committee that would eventually become the Hospital Ethics Committee. Shortly thereafter, and in agreement with a comatose patient's family and other physicians, I turned off a respirator for the first time. Several relatives and I stood by the bedside as the patient's respiration and pulse ceased; but we had not turned off the cardiac monitor and we watched in awe as the electrical conduction waves of the heart continued undiminished long after all respiration and pulse had ceased. We knew that the patient had no hope of recovery. We knew that he would not have wanted his life prolonged by artificial means. We knew that it was ethical and legal to end artificial life support. Yet the sheer vitality of that cardiac wave made us doubt our decision. I learned that the very data we acquire in the intensive care setting has the capacity to question our certainties.

> *I had to experience my father's death to admit my own mortality.*

In subsequent years I attended conferences, and read in and eventually taught Bioethics. The names of Quinlan, Conroy, Brother Fox, Bartlet, Bouvia, Salkewicz, and Cruzan became part of my intellectual life as did the writings of Fletcher, Marsh, Pellegrino, Jonsen, Engelhardt, Siegler, Callahan, Rachels, Quill, and so many others. I learned the principles of biomedical ethics as espoused by Beachamp and Childress, understood Aristotle's respect for equals, and became familiar with Locke and Hume. Yet I was still unprepared for the letter written to me by my friend Tom, a retired professor who was increasingly disabled by multiple sclerosis. He asked for my assistance in ending his life at some undefined time in the future. We met one long afternoon at his apartment to discuss his request; but while I recognized his right to choose the time of his own death, I found that I could not accede to his request. Later he would return home to die after refusing surgery for an intestinal obstruction. I suspect that he took his own life and regret that, while I did not feel that I could provide him with the means, I was not able to be with him in his final, lonely moments.

He asked for my assistance in ending his life. . . .
While I recognized his right to choose the time of his
own death, I found that I could not accede to his
request.

A few months later a 26-year-old woman, on mechanical ventilation for multiple sclerosis, made a request of her doctors and the Ethics Committee to end all life support treatment. We met with her and her pastor and family and came to the conclusion that, for her, this was a rational choice. Some days later her physician ordered her respiratory support turned off. I happened by chance to pass by her room and she was gasping and struggling for air in a long slow process of dying. No one had thought, or were perhaps afraid to think, of easing her final hours with morphine. Her struggle taught me that the responsibility for ending a treatment did not absolve a physician of the obligation to ease painful suffering.

Some time later a woman in her 60s came to our hospital when her funds ran out and she could no longer afford her private physician. Exhausted and in pain from a metastatic malignancy, she arrived in the emergency room with her mother and daughter. She begged me to promise to allow her to die with as little pain as possible but not to do any more tests or procedures. After consultation with her previous physician and a perusal of her records, I agreed; we admitted her and cared for her for the week prior to her death without a single X-ray, blood test, or surgical intervention. The three women, each a mother and daughter, created bonds within which the patient was cradled, nurtured, protected from our aggressive insistence, and allowed to die in peace.

Requests from AIDS patients

A flood of deaths now followed, mostly from AIDS, for we were right in the middle of the epidemic. The first patient I met with AIDS was a colleague and personal friend. Yet I sensed a gulf between us, created by my own conformity, fear, and prejudice that I could not bridge. A great choreographer, he was memorialized by his colleagues in a ceremony that left me stunned, in tears, and ashamed. A year later another gay patient called to ask me for help. I at first avoided direct responsibility, arguing that I was not a specialist in infectious disease and arranged for his care with another physician. As his disease went from bad to worse, he developed a ferocious and intractable headache that did not respond to treatment for infection or lymphoma. Visiting him often at home and every day in the hospital, I gradually assumed the role of primary physician without ever realizing that it had happened. Toward the end he decided that he wanted to go home to die. We agreed to his request and sent him home to his family. To ease his ferocious pain he required constant morphine, but fortunately he died within a few days. In a sense his agony and suffering first shamed and then liberated me. The courage of these two men had made me a healthier person and prepared me to be a better physician.

AIDS deaths became all too common. A marvelous man, a television and theater costume designer, met each day with the most extraordinary religious faith. My visits to his home left me feeling that his company was a gift. I watched a jazz musician die in a coma, the bed shaking uncontrollably with grand mal seizures. Despite the best of consultation and a variety of drugs, we could not get the movement disorder under control. His sister, standing next to me at the bedside, begged me to end his life. But I could not, constrained by law and custom, and by ethical principles. These and other patients often experienced pain that could only be controlled by inducing coma. A few could not be relieved at all, their suffering due almost entirely to their total loss of dignity and autonomy. This realization has greatly shaken my certainty that it is always the physician's duty to save and not to end a patient's life.

I know that being alive is not the same as having a life.

Recently I have had no less than three rational, competent elderly men and women assert that when the time came they did not want their life to continue in pain, in suffering, or without dignity and independence. I sat and listened to each one not knowing how to answer. My encounters with death have changed me, but I remain uncertain of what is right. I know that being alive is not the same as having a life. But I also know that we can be corrupted by not easing suffering, perhaps almost as much as by killing a patient. We need a philosophy and an ethic that allows each of us to die with dignity and in peace. I hope that the future allows me to have a better understanding of these dilemmas.

5

Physician-Assisted Suicide Is Immoral

Daniel P. Sulmasy

Daniel P. Sulmasy, a Franciscan brother, is an assistant professor of medicine and a research scholar at the Center for Clinical Bioethics at Georgetown University Medical Center, Washington, D.C. He has published many scholarly articles on medical ethics.

Killing patients or helping them commit suicide is always morally wrong. Withholding or withdrawing treatment from terminally ill patients and allowing them to die can be moral, as long as it is not the physician's intent to cause death. Each human life has an intrinsic value that must always be respected and revered. It is immoral to intentionally end a life.

We live in a curious world. The most famous physician on the planet is now Dr. Jack Kevorkian, who makes a living helping people commit suicide. Efforts are afoot in several states to allow doctors legally to help kill their patients. In November of 1994, for example, with little fanfare, the voters of Oregon passed the world's first law to make it legal for doctors to help patients commit suicide. The law—now blocked by a federal court ruling—requires doctors who participate to prescribe a "safe lethal dose." Questions about how a dose could be both safe and lethal at the same time seem to escape the authors of the bill. The world, as Alice in Wonderland once said, gets curiouser and curiouser. [In October 1997, the Supreme Court upheld the Oregon law; in November 1997, Oregon voters elected to keep the law.]

Many people have become confused by this curious debate about physician-assisted suicide and euthanasia. Some have been led to believe (falsely) that they and their loved ones will be forced to make a cruel choice at the end of life: either languish for months on a torturous ventilator or swallow a few dozen pills and end it all. But this view is wrong—dead wrong. My aim in this article is to help explain the morality of allowing patients to die—a middle course between purposeless treatment on the one hand and euthanasia or suicide on the other.

From Daniel P. Sulmasy, "Death with Dignity: A Franciscan Doctor's Perspective," *St. Anthony Messenger*, January 1996. Reprinted with permission.

Since most deaths in America are now preceded by a decision to withhold or withdraw some form of treatment, you probably have had personal experience here. My own grandfather died while I was an intern, just out of medical school. I helped my mother come to the decision not to put him on a ventilator and not to attempt cardiopulmonary resuscitation when his heart stopped. These decisions were hard ones, but they seemed morally correct, and were perfectly permissible under Church teaching. Yet it would *not* have seemed morally correct to have given my grandfather an injection of a rapidly acting poison. We let Poppy die, but we didn't kill him. What explains the moral difference between these two actions?

History can help to illuminate our question, but only if the historical facts are accurately understood. Unfortunately, many people (including many doctors) are confused about what ancient doctors like Hippocrates had to say about killing and allowing to die. The Hippocratic Oath is the traditional standard of medicine.

First, it is important to realize that the Hippocratic Oath does *not* say that physicians must continue to treat patients and keep them alive no matter what. The oath says, "I will use treatment to help the sick according to my ability and judgment." This *clearly* does not mean keep treating until the treatment kills the patient.

Second, Hippocrates also says that physicians should "refuse to treat those who are overmastered by their disease, realizing that in such cases medicine is powerless."

Third, the Oath of Hippocrates expressly prohibits euthanasia and assisted suicide, saying, "I will not give poison to anyone though asked to do so, nor will I suggest such a plan." So, it seems fair to say that Hippocrates at least implicitly accepted the idea of a distinction between killing and allowing to die.

From the earliest days, Christians considered suicide and euthanasia sinful. However, by the 16th century, long before there were ventilators or intensive-care units, Catholic theologians developed the distinction between *ordinary* and *extraordinary* means. They taught that Christians had a moral obligation to preserve their lives in the face of illness, but that they were not required to go to extraordinary lengths to do so.

My aim in this article is to help explain the morality of allowing patients to die.

If a 16th-century doctor said that moving to the mountains would be best for a patient's health, and moving to the mountains would require leaving family and friends and losing the immediate family's savings, the patient was under no obligation to do so. Therefore, by the time there *were* things like ventilators around, it was easy for Pope Pius XII to say in 1957 that such treatments might present the patient with an "extraordinary" burden, and it would therefore be morally permissible to forgo such treatment.

Thus the Church distinguished clearly between killing patients by suicide or euthanasia (which has never been permissible), and allowing them to die by withholding or withdrawing life-supporting treatments (which has been seen as permissible in the right circumstances).

Philosophers have recently attacked this distinction between killing and allowing to die, arguing that it is unsound. Some of their arguments have helped to make matters clearer. Others have left the picture even more confused.

One might be tempted to say that the difference between killing and allowing to die lies in the fact that killing is always active while allowing to die is always passive. Yet most people would agree that disconnecting a dying patient from a ventilator—an *act*—is a classical case of allowing to die. One actively turns *off* a switch or actively *disconnects* a piece of tubing. So the difference between killing and allowing to die can't just be the difference between active and passive.

Second, one might suggest that, in killing, *a person* causes the patient's death, but in allowing to die *nature* causes the death. But it is hard to say that the one who disconnects a life-support system is not in some sense causing death. If the patient needs a continuous infusion of a medicine to maintain blood pressure, and the doctor turns a stopcock, the medicine stops, the blood pressure drops, and the patient goes into shock and dies, can the doctor seriously claim to have played no causal role in the death?

The Hippocratic Oath does not *say that physicians must continue to treat patients and keep them alive no matter what.*

Even if one *could* adequately describe the difference between killing and allowing to die, it is argued, the distinction wouldn't make a *moral* difference. Let me illustrate my point with two case studies from philosopher and euthanasia proponent James Rachels:

"Smith stands to gain a large inheritance if anything should happen to his six-year-old cousin. One evening while the child is taking his bath, Smith sneaks into the bathroom and drowns the child, and then arranges things to make it look like an accident. No one is the wiser, and Smith gets his inheritance.

"Jones also stands to gain if anything should happen to his six-year-old cousin. Like Smith, Jones sneaks in planning to drown the child in his bath. However, just as he enters the bathroom Jones sees the child slip, hit his head and fall face-down in the water. Jones is delighted; he stands by, ready to push the child's head back down under if necessary, but it is not necessary. With only a little thrashing about, the child drowns all by himself, 'accidentally,' as Jones watches and does nothing. No one is the wiser, and Jones gets his inheritance."

So, it seems as if Smith killed his cousin and Jones allowed his cousin to die. *But,* Rachels asks, does this make a moral difference? He would answer no.

I want to argue that there is an important logical mistake in Rachels's question. He would be right (there would be no moral distinction) if you could agree that all acts of killing are morally wrong, and all acts of allowing to die are morally right. But that's not what either traditional medicine or Catholic teaching holds. Catholic understanding makes distinctions among situations where death is imminent. Catholic understanding would say it like this: All acts of killing patients are morally wrong. Some acts of allowing them to die are also morally wrong, and some are not.

The difference between killing and allowing to die can't just be the difference between active and passive.

Once one understands the distinction between killing and allowing to die, the stories of Smith and Jones can be seen as *illustrations* of the distinction, not as a refutation. All acts of killing are morally wrong, and so Smith is clearly wrong. Some acts of allowing to die are morally wrong, and some are not. Jones's story just falls into the category of acts of allowing to die that are morally wrong. That's plain to see.

Here is how I would phrase the distinction between killing and allowing to die: *Killing is an act in which someone performs an action that gives the victim a new fatal disease with the intention of thereby causing the patient's death. Allowing to die is an act in which someone either performs an action to remove a treatment for a pre-existing fatal disease or refrains from action that would treat a pre-existing fatal disease.*

If I kill a patient by a lethal injection, I act and create a new and fatal disease that the patient didn't have before. If I do so intending that the patient should die as a result, that is always wrong. If I allow that same person to die (whether by removing ventilator treatment for a fatal disease called respiratory failure, or by refraining from starting ventilator treatment), this is sometimes wrong and sometimes right. Each instance requires careful consideration.

Intention is the key

What, then, explains the wrongness that all acts of killing patients have in common with the *wrong* acts of allowing to die? The answer is one word: *intention*. Anyone who kills a patient *intends* that the patient should die by way of that action. This is what makes killing wrong. If one allows a patient to die with the specific intention that the patient should die by way of that action (the patient might have lived otherwise), this is also wrong. This allowing to die is not to be confused with allowing a natural death, as we will see below.

In killing (or in physician-assisted suicide), the doctor intends the death of the patient. Just as Smith acts wrongly by drowning his cousin, so does the physician who gives a lethal injection. Nonetheless, *some* acts of allowing to die are also morally wrong—those in which the doctor's intention is the death of the patient.

So, for example, because Jones intends that his cousin should die in order for him to collect the inheritance, Jones is morally in the wrong. In the same way, if a doctor disconnects the ventilator from a patient with the explicit intention that the patient should die so that he and the patient's wife can run off together with the insurance money, that physician has also acted wrongly.

On the other hand, if the doctor disconnects the ventilator intending simply that the patient should not be on the ventilator (perhaps because it is useless in preventing inevitable death), that physician has not acted wrongly. This is *good* allowing to die. It is perfectly morally permissible.

Intention plays a key role here, as it does in much of morality. But intentions, of course, are hard to know. Sometimes one does not even understand one's own intentions. And it is precisely because intentions are so difficult to know that the distinction between killing and allowing to die is so important.

All acts of killing patients are morally wrong. Some acts of allowing them to die are also morally wrong, and some are not.

Killing is usually easy to recognize. Injecting poison into a patient's veins is a pretty straightforward act. It would be hard to argue that one's intentions did not include the death of the patient if one were to inject a poison. The burden of proof is overwhelmingly on a killer to explain how it was a mistake (or the killer was deceived or drugged) so that the action would not really be intentional. It is therefore very useful to be able to distinguish acts of killing from acts of allowing to die: We know that killing, in the case of physicians treating patients, is always wrong.

This is not the case with allowing to die. If I unplug a ventilator, how does anyone know what my intentions were? It might even be hard for me to know. Nonetheless, one can apply a simple (if imperfect) check on one's intentions. One can ask, how would one feel if the patient were not to die after one's action? Would one feel that one had failed to accomplish what one had set out to do? Or would one be open to the possibility that the patient might survive? If one's honest answer is that one would not feel frustrated, but would be open to the possibility that the patient might survive, then the patient's death was probably not one's intention.

Consider the paradigm case of allowing to die: turning off the ventilator for Karen Ann Quinlan. As is well known, Ms. Quinlan did not die when her family finally won the court's approval and turned off the ventilator, even though her death was expected. But no one then tried to strangle her. Their intention was simply that Karen's death not be prevented by a ventilator. As it turned out, the ventilator was not preventing her death. She lived on for several years.

Intention isn't desire

It is particularly important not to confuse desire with intention. Many who object to moral arguments based upon intentions have mistaken *intention* for *desire*. To show why intending something is not the same as desiring it, consider some examples. I can, for instance, intend to do what I do not desire (for example, going to see my patients when I am tired and would rather not). I can also desire to do what I do not intend (I may desire to eat a high-cholesterol diet but never form an intention to act that way lest my patients think me a hypocrite). Desiring something is not the same as intending to make it happen.

Nor should one feel guilty about wanting loved ones to pass away quickly when they are close to death and suffering. I, for one, have certainly desired that some of my patients would die quickly after I have withdrawn life support. In many cases I have hoped for their quick death; even prayed that God would take them. But this does not mean that I *intended* their death. Yes, I desired their hasty death, but the taking of the life was God's.

Medicine has traditionally prohibited the intentional death of patients. But medicine does not want patients to be prisoners of technology. The traditional morality that has permitted withholding and withdrawing "extraordinary" care *presupposes* this distinction between killing and allowing to die. Patients should not suffer needlessly. If the treatment is of no benefit, or if the burdens of treatment are disproportionate to the expected benefits, one may withhold or withdraw that treatment. But the intention in doing so must simply be that the useless or burdensome treatment be withdrawn. What one cannot intend is that there should be no such human life.

Why intending death is wrong

Christians recognize life as a gift from God. Human life, taking God as its image and likeness, has a special worth or dignity. Believing that life has such dignity, one can never hold the destruction of that dignity as one's intention.

There was once a time when human life had intrinsic meaning; its value seemed intuitively obvious even to nonbelievers. Such a moral intuition can no longer be taken for granted.

One can argue that, without religion, human beings are inherently communal beings. The value of human life is held in trust by a web of relationships. One can therefore argue that suicide is a rejection of relationships—a violent severing of one's connections with one's fellow human beings.

Some might make the claim that life loses its value when freedom and control are gone. But every human life depends upon others, and that dependency does not diminish dignity. Some of the most important things about being human, like birth and mortality, are beyond human control. One cannot, by force of will, live a life free of all suffering.

There was once a time when human life had intrinsic meaning.

One will never be able to choose one's biological parents, no matter how much success genetic engineering has. Further, human life does not appear to lose its value when freedom and control are taken away. One of my favorite portraits of dignity is a photo of the Rev. Dr. Martin Luther King, Jr., in an Alabama prison cell. Acts of injustice deny but cannot eradicate the intrinsic value of human life.

Of course, human meaning and value are not infinite. On a cosmic scale, human life seems small, frail and fallible. One need only believe that each human life has a *high* intrinsic value, and that this dignity is the same for everyone. The value of human life cannot be said to admit of degrees. To say so is to say that some people's lives are more valuable than others'. If all human lives have intrinsic meaning and value, then to intend someone's death is to deny that the dying person's life has such value. But humans are finite; death is a part of life. Since that person's value is not infinite, one can sometimes let go of that life by allowing to die. What one can never do is to claim the right to destroy it.

Allow me to summarize: There *is* a moral difference between killing and allowing to die. All killing of patients is morally wrong, while allowing some patients to die is not. The moral evaluation of these acts is based upon intention. Belief in this distinction allows a middle course between suicide and euthanasia on the one hand, and lingering on a ventilator on the other. Patients need not be overmastered by technology, and can stop treatments that are ineffective or excessively burdensome. But neither do they need to be overmastered by the despair, hopelessness and fear that lead some to kill themselves or to ask to be killed.

Euthanasia is not death with dignity, nor is dying alone with a plastic bag over one's head, spitting up the pills one has tried to force down one's own throat. Killing is the ultimate indignity. To be allowed to die in the company of loved ones, reminded that as one passes away into the mystery of death, one's life has meaning and value in the eyes of God, family and community, even in the face of dependency and pain, is real death with dignity. Killing and allowing to die are not the same.

6

Physician-Assisted Suicide Is a Constitutional Right

Ronald Dworkin, Thomas Nagel, Robert Nozick, John Rawls, Thomas Scanlon, and Judith Jarvis Thomson

Ronald Dworkin is professor of jurisprudence at Oxford University and professor of law and of philosophy at New York University. He is the author of Life's Dominion *and* Freedom's Law: The Moral Reading of the Constitution. *Robert Nozick, John Rawls, and Thomas Scanlon teach at Harvard University, Thomas Nagel at New York University, and Judith Jarvis Thomson at MIT.*

Editor's note: In June 1997, the Supreme Court ruled on two cases in which state laws against physician-assisted suicide were challenged as unconstitutional.[1] The Court upheld the laws, effectively refusing to grant Americans a constitutional right to physician-assisted suicide. The following two-part viewpoint presents a brief filed as amicus curiae in these cases by six moral philosophers. Part I is an introduction to the brief by Ronald Dworkin, one of the six philosophers. Part II is the brief itself.

Individuals have a constitutionally protected right to autonomously make the most intimate choices and decisions regarding their lives, including the choice to end their lives. This right not only stems from the original statements of individual liberty and freedom found in the Constitution, but is also supported by previous Supreme Court decisions. For example, in *Planned Parenthood vs. Casey*, the high court determined that people have a right to make their own decisions about matters "involving the most intimate and personal choices a person may make in a lifetime, choices central to personal dignity and autonomy." The Constitution clearly prohibits government from imposing any ethical or religious beliefs on individuals, including moral judgments about suicide.

From Ronald Dworkin, Thomas Nagel, Robert Nozick, John Rawls, Thomas Scanlon, and Judith Jarvis Thomson, "Assisted Suicide: The Philosophers' Brief," *New York Review of Books*, March 27, 1997. Reprinted with permission.

I

We cannot be sure, until the Supreme Court decides the assisted suicide cases and its decision is published, how far the justices might have accepted or rejected the arguments of the brief published below.[2] In this introduction I shall describe the oral argument before them last January, and offer some suggestions about how, if they decide against the brief's position, as many commentators now think they will, they might do the least damage to constitutional law.

The laws of all but one American state now forbid doctors to prescribe lethal pills for patients who want to kill themselves.[3] These cases began when groups of dying patients and their doctors in Washington State and New York each sued asking that these prohibitions be declared unconstitutional so that the patients could be given, when and if they asked for it, medicine to hasten their death. The pleadings described the agony in which the patient plaintiffs were dying, and two federal Circuit Courts of Appeal—the Ninth Circuit in the Washington case and the Second Circuit in the New York case—agreed with the plaintiffs that the Constitution forbids the government from flatly prohibiting doctors to help end such desperate and pointless suffering.[4]

Washington State and New York appealed these decisions to the Supreme Court, and a total of sixty amicus briefs were filed, including briefs on behalf of the American Medical Association and the United States Catholic Conference urging the Court to reverse the circuit court decisions, and on behalf of the American Medical Students Association and the Gay Men's Health Crisis urging it to affirm them. The justices' comments during oral argument persuaded many observers that the Court would reverse the decisions, probably by a lopsided majority. The justices repeatedly cited two versions—one theoretical, the other practical—of the "slippery slope" argument: that it would be impossible to limit a right to assisted suicide in an acceptable way, once that right was recognized.

The theoretical version of the argument denies that any principled line can be drawn between cases in which proponents say a right of assisted suicide is appropriate and those in which they concede that it is not. The circuit courts recognized only a right for competent patients already dying in great physical pain to have pills prescribed that they could take themselves. Several justices asked on what grounds the right once granted could be so severely limited. Why should it be denied to dying patients who are so feeble or paralyzed that they cannot take pills themselves and who beg a doctor to inject a lethal drug into them? Or to patients who are not dying but face years of intolerable physical or emotional pain, or crippling paralysis or dependence? But if the right were extended that far, on what ground could it be denied to anyone who had formed a desire to die—to a sixteen-year-old suffering from a severe case of unrequited love, for example?

Defining the argument

The philosophers' brief answers these questions in two steps. First, it defines a very general moral and constitutional principle—that every competent person has the right to make momentous personal decisions which invoke fundamental religious or philosophical convictions about life's value for himself. Second, it recognizes that people may make such momentous decisions impulsively or out of emotional depression, when their act does not reflect their enduring convictions; and it therefore allows that in some circumstances a state has the constitutional power to override that right in order to protect citizens from mistaken but irrevocable acts of self-destruction. States may be allowed to prevent assisted suicide by people who—it is plausible to think—would later be grateful if they were prevented from dying.

That two-step argument would justify a state's protecting a disappointed adolescent from himself. It would equally plainly not justify forcing a competent dying patient to live in agony a few weeks longer. People will of course disagree about the cases in between these extremes, and if the Court adopted this argument, the federal courts would no doubt be faced with a succession of cases in years to come testing whether, for example, it is plausible to assume that a desperately crippled patient in constant pain but with years to live, who has formed a settled and repeatedly stated wish to die, would one day be glad he was forced to stay alive. But though two justices dwelled, during the oral argument, on the unappealing prospect of a series of such cases coming before the courts, it seems better that the courts do assume that burden, which they could perhaps mitigate through careful rulings, than that they be relieved of it at the cost of such terrible suffering.

Two federal Circuit Courts of Appeal . . . [agreed] that the Constitution forbids the government from flatly prohibiting doctors to help end such desperate and pointless suffering.

The practical version of the slippery slope argument is more complex. If assisted suicide were permitted in principle, every state would presumably adopt regulations to insure that a patient's decision for suicide is informed, competent, and free. But many people fear that such regulations could not be adequately enforced, and that particularly vulnerable patients—poor patients dying in overcrowded hospitals that had scarce resources, for example—might be pressured or hustled into a decision for death they would not otherwise make. The evidence suggests, however, that such patients might be better rather than less well protected if assisted suicide were legalized with appropriate safeguards.

More of them could then benefit from relief that is already available—illegally—to more fortunate people who have established relationships with doctors willing to run the risks of helping them to die. The current two-tier system—a chosen death and an end of pain outside the law for those with connections and stony refusals for most other people—is one of the greatest scandals of contemporary medical practice. The sense many middle-class people have that if necessary their own doctor "will know what to do" helps to explain why the political pressure is not stronger for a fairer and more open system in which the law acknowledges for everyone what influential people now expect for themselves.

For example, in a recent study in the state of Washington, which guaranteed respondents anonymity, 26 percent of doctors surveyed said they had received explicit requests for help in dying, and had provided, overall, lethal prescriptions to 24 percent of patients requesting them.[5] In other studies, 40 percent of Michigan oncologists surveyed reported that patients had initiated requests for death, 18 percent said they had participated in assisted suicide, and 4 percent in "active euthanasia"—injecting lethal drugs themselves. In San Francisco, 53 percent of the 1,995 responding physicians said they had granted an AIDS patient's request for suicide assistance at least once.[6] These statistics approach the rates at which doctors help patients die in Holland, where assisted suicide is in effect legal.

Better care for patients

The most important benefit of legalized assisted suicide for poor patients, however, might be better care while they live. For though the medical experts cited in various briefs disagreed sharply about the percentage of terminal cases in which pain can be made tolerable through advanced and expensive palliative techniques, they did not disagree that a great many patients do not receive the relief they could have. The Solicitor General who urged the Court to reverse the lower court judgments conceded in the oral argument that 25 percent of terminally ill patients actually do die in pain. That appalling figure is the result of several factors, including medical ignorance and fear of liability, inadequate hospital funding, and (as the Solicitor General suggested) the failure of insurers and health care programs to cover the cost of special hospice care. Better training in palliative medicine, and legislation requiring such coverage, would obviously improve the situation, but it seems perverse to argue that the patients who would be helped were better pain management available must die horribly because it is not; and, as Justice Breyer pointed out, the number of patients in that situation might well increase as medical costs continue to escalate.

Patients might be better rather than less well protected if assisted suicide were legalized with appropriate safeguards.

According to several briefs, moreover, patients whose pain is either uncontrollable or uncontrolled are often "terminally sedated"—intravenous drugs (usually barbiturates or benzodiazepines) are injected to induce a pharmacologic coma during which the patient is given neither water nor nutrition and dies sooner than he otherwise would.[7] Terminal sedation is widely accepted as legal, though it advances death.[8] But it is not subject to regulations nearly as stringent as those that a state forced to allow assisted suicide would enact, because such regulations would presumably include a requirement that hospitals, before accepting any request for assistance in suicide, must demonstrate that effective medical care including state-of-the-art pain management had been offered. The guidelines recently published by a network of ethics committees in the Bay Area of California, for example, among other stringent safeguards, provide that a primary care physician who receives a request for suicide must make an initial referral to a hospice program or to a physician experienced in palliative care, and certify in a formal report filed in a state registry, signed by an independent second physician with expertise in such care, that the best available pain relief has been offered to the patient.[9]

Doctors and hospitals anxious to avoid expense would have very little incentive to begin a process that would focus attention on their palliative care practices. They would be more likely to continue the widespread practice of relatively inexpensive terminal care which is supplemented, perhaps, with terminal sedation. It is at least possible, however, that patients' knowledge of the possibility of assisted suicide would make it more difficult for such doctors to continue as before. That is the view of the Coalition of Hospice Professionals, who said, in their own amicus brief, "Indeed, removing legal bans on suicide assistance will enhance the opportunity for advanced hospice care for all patients because regulation of physician-assisted suicide would mandate that all palliative measures be exhausted as a condition precedent to assisted suicide."

The Supreme Court

So neither version of the slippery slope argument seems very strong. It is nevertheless understandable that Supreme Court justices are reluctant, particularly given how little experience we have so far with legalized assisted suicide, to declare that all but one of the states must change their laws to allow a practice many citizens think abominable and sacrilegious. But as the philosophers' brief that follows emphasizes, the Court is in an unusually difficult position. If it closes the door to a constitutional right to assisted suicide it will do substantial damage to constitutional practice and precedent, as well as to thousands of people in great suffering. It would face a dilemma in justifying any such decision, because it would be forced to choose between the two unappealing strategies that the brief describes.

The first strategy—declaring that terminally ill patients in great pain do not have a constitutional right to control their own death, even in principle—seems alien to our constitutional system, as the Solicitor General himself insisted in the oral argument. It would also undermine a variety of the Court's own past decisions, including the carefully constructed position on abortion set out in its 1993 decision in *Planned Parenthood* v. *Casey*. Indeed some amicus briefs took the occasion of the assisted suicide cases to criticize the abortion decisions—a brief filed on behalf of Senator Orrin Hatch of Utah and Representatives Henry Hyde of Illinois and Charles Canady of Florida, for example, declared that the abortion decisions were "of questionable legitimacy and even more questionable prudence." Protecting the abortion rulings was presumably one of the aims of the Clinton administration in arguing, through the Solicitor General, for the second strategy instead.

The first strategy would create an even more evident inconsistency within the practice of terminal medicine itself. Since the *Cruzan* v. *Missouri* decision discussed in the brief, lawyers have generally assumed that the Court would protect the right of any competent patient to have life sustaining equipment removed from his body even though he would then die. In the oral argument, several justices suggested a "common-sense" distinction between the moral significance of acts, on the one hand, and omissions, on the other. This distinction, they suggested, would justify a constitutional distinction between prescribing lethal pills and removing life support; for, in their view, removing support is only a matter of "letting nature take its course," while prescribing pills is an active intervention that brings death sooner than natural processes would.

Terminal sedation is widely accepted as legal, though it advances death.

The discussion of this issue in the philosophers' brief is therefore particularly significant. The brief insists that such suggestions wholly misunderstand the "common-sense" distinction, which is not between acts and omissions, but between acts or omissions that are designed to cause death and those that are not. One justice suggested that a patient who insists that life support be disconnected is not committing suicide. That is wrong: he is committing suicide if he aims at death, as most such patients do, just as someone whose wrist is cut in an accident is committing suicide if he refuses to try to stop the bleeding. The distinction between acts that aim at death and those that do not cannot justify a constitutional distinction between assisting in suicide and terminating life support. Some doctors, who stop life support only because the patient so demands, do not aim at death. But neither do doctors who prescribe lethal pills only for the same reason, and hope that the patient does not take them. And many doctors who terminate life support obviously do aim at death, including those who deny nutrition during terminal sedation, because denying nutrition is designed to hasten death, not to relieve pain.

The power of the state

There are equally serious objections, however, to the second strategy the philosophers' brief discusses. This strategy concedes a general right to assisted suicide but holds that states have the power to judge that the risks of allowing any exercise of that right are too great. It is obviously dangerous for the Court to allow a state to deny a constitutional right on the ground that the state lacks the will or resource to enforce safeguards if it is exercised, particularly when the case for the practical version of the "slippery slope" objection seems so weak and has been little examined. As Justice William Rehnquist, who perhaps favors the first strategy, observed in the oral argument, "[I]f we assume a liberty interest but nevertheless say that, even assuming a liberty interest, a state can prohibit it entirely, that would be rather a conundrum."[10]

If the justices believe that they cannot now accept the lower court decisions, in spite of the powerful defense offered by the respondents and the various briefs supporting them, then they should consider a third strategy—postponement. They might declare that both precedent and principle offer strong grounds for a constitutional right to manage one's own death, but that there is as yet too little experience with legally permitted assisted suicide for the Court to rule that states lack the constitutional power to follow their traditional practice of outlawing it.

That third strategy, unlike the first two, would in effect commit the Court to considering a new challenge in the future when a much more substantial record of experience is available—from Oregon and any other American state that follows its lead in permitting assisted suicide by legislation, and from the Netherlands, Switzerland, the Northern Territories of Australia, and any other jurisdiction whose legislature takes the same course. In the meantime, the public would have had an opportunity to participate more fully in the argument about principle; and, when circumstances make it possible, wide public discussion is a desirable and democratic preliminary to a final Supreme Court adjudication.[11] Postponement is not what the philosophers' brief urges. But it would be the most statesmanlike way in which the Court could make the wrong decision.

—*Ronald Dworkin*

II

Amici are six moral and political philosophers who differ on many issues of public morality and policy. They are united, however, in their conviction that respect for fundamental principles of liberty and justice, as well as for the American constitutional tradition, requires that the decisions of the Courts of Appeals be affirmed.

Introduction and summary of argument

These cases do not invite or require the Court to make moral, ethical, or religious judgments about how people should approach or confront their death or about when it is ethically appropriate to hasten one's own death or to ask others for help in doing so. On the contrary, they ask the Court to recognize that individuals have a constitutionally protected interest in making those grave judgments for themselves, free from the imposition of any religious or philosophical orthodoxy by court or legislature. States have a constitutionally legitimate interest in protecting individuals from irrational, ill-informed, pressured, or unstable decisions to hasten their own death. To that end, states may regulate and limit the assistance that doctors may give individuals who express a wish to die. But states may not deny people in the position of the patient-plaintiffs in these cases the opportunity to demonstrate, through whatever reasonable procedures the state might institute—even procedures that err on the side of caution— that their decision to die is indeed informed, stable, and fully free. Denying that opportunity to terminally ill patients who are in agonizing pain or otherwise doomed to an existence they regard as intolerable could only be justified on the basis of a religious or ethical conviction about the value or meaning of life itself. Our Constitution forbids government to impose such convictions on its citizens. Petitioners [i.e., the state authorities of Washington and New York] and the amici who support them offer two contradictory arguments. Some deny that the patient-plaintiffs have any constitutionally protected liberty interest in hastening their own deaths. But that liberty interest flows directly from this Court's previous decisions. It flows from the right of people to make their own decisions about matters "involving the most intimate and personal choices a person may make in a lifetime, choices central to personal dignity and autonomy." *Planned Parenthood* v. *Casey*, 505 U.S. 833, 851 (1992).

Some [authorities] deny that the patient-plaintiffs have any constitutionally protected liberty interest in hastening their own deaths.

The Solicitor General, urging reversal in support of Petitioners, recognizes that the patient-plaintiffs do have a constitutional liberty interest at stake in these cases. *See* Brief for the United States as Amicus Curiae Supporting Petitioners at 12, *Washington* v. *Vacco* [hereinafter Brief for the United States] ("The term 'liberty' in the Due Process Clause . . . is broad enough to encompass an interest on the part of terminally ill, mentally competent adults in obtaining relief from the kind of suffering experienced by the plaintiffs in this case, which includes not only severe physical pain, but also the despair and distress that comes from physical deterioration and the inability to control basic bodily functions."); *see also id.* at 13 ("*Cruzan* . . . supports the conclusion that a liberty interest is at stake in this case.").

The Solicitor General nevertheless argues that Washington and New York properly ignored this profound interest when they required the patient-plaintiffs to live on in circumstances they found intolerable. He argues that a state may simply declare that it is unable to devise a regulatory scheme that would adequately protect patients whose desire to die might be ill-informed or unstable or foolish or not fully free, and that a state may therefore fall back on a blanket prohibition. This Court has never accepted that patently dangerous rationale for denying protection altogether to a conceded fundamental constitutional interest. It would be a serious mistake to do so now. If that rationale were accepted, an interest acknowledged to be constitutionally protected would be rendered empty.

Argument

I. The Liberty Interest Asserted Here Is Protected by the Due Process Clause

The Due Process Clause of the Fourteenth Amendment protects the liberty interest asserted by the patient-plaintiffs here.

Certain decisions are momentous in their impact on the character of a person's life—decisions about religious faith, political and moral allegiance, marriage, procreation, and death, for example. Such deeply personal decisions pose controversial questions about how and why human life has value. In a free society, individuals must be allowed to make those decisions for themselves, out of their own faith, conscience, and convictions. This Court has insisted, in a variety of contexts and circumstances, that this great freedom is among those protected by the Due Process Clause as essential to a community of "ordered liberty." *Palko* v. *Connecticut*, 302 U.S. 319, 325 (1937). In its recent decision in *Planned Par-*

enthood v. *Casey*, 505 U.S. 833, 851 (1992), the Court offered a paradigmatic statement of that principle:

> matters [ ] involving the most intimate and personal choices a person may make in a lifetime, choices central to a person's dignity and autonomy, are central to the liberty protected by the Fourteenth Amendment.

That declaration reflects an idea underlying many of our basic constitutional protections.[1] As the Court explained in *West Virginia State Board of Education* v. *Barnette*, 319 U.S. 624, 642 (1943):

> If there is any fixed star in our constitutional constellation, it is that no official . . . can prescribe what shall be orthodox in politics, nationalism, religion, or other matters of opinion or force citizens to confess by word or act their faith therein.

A person's interest in following his own convictions at the end of life is so central a part of the more general right to make "intimate and personal choices" for himself that a failure to protect that particular interest would undermine the general right altogether. Death is, for each of us, among the most significant events of life. As the Chief Justice said in *Cruzan* v. *Missouri*, 497 U.S. 261, 281 (1990), "[t]he choice between life and death is a deeply personal decision of obvious and overwhelming finality." Most of us see death—whatever we think will follow it—as the final act of life's drama, and we want that last act to reflect our own convictions, those we have tried to live by, not the convictions of others forced on us in our most vulnerable moment.

It is certainly not permissible for a doctor to kill one patient in order to use his organs to save another.

Different people, of different religious and ethical beliefs, embrace very different convictions about which way of dying confirms and which contradicts the value of their lives. Some fight against death with every weapon their doctors can devise. Others will do nothing to hasten death even if they pray it will come soon. Still others, including the patient-plaintiffs in these cases, want to end their lives when they think that living on, in the only way they can, would disfigure rather than enhance the lives they had created. Some people make the latter choice not just to escape pain. Even if it were possible to eliminate all pain for a dying patient—and frequently that is not possible—that would not end or even much alleviate the anguish some would feel at remaining alive, but intubated, helpless, and often sedated near oblivion.

None of these dramatically different attitudes about the meaning of death can be dismissed as irrational. None should be imposed, either by the pressure of doctors or relatives or by the fiat of government, on people who reject it. Just as it would be intolerable for government to dictate that doctors never be permitted to try to keep someone alive as long as possible, when that is what the patient wishes, so it is intolerable for government to dictate that doctors may never, under any circumstances, help someone to die who believes that further life means only degradation. The Constitution insists that people must be free to make these deeply personal decisions for themselves and must not be forced to end their lives in a way that appalls them, just because that is what some majority thinks proper.

Since patients have a right not to have life-support machinery attached to their bodies, they have, in principle, a right to compel its removal.

II. This Court's Decisions in Casey *and* Cruzan *Compel Recognition of a Liberty Interest Here*
A. Casey *Supports the Liberty Interest Asserted Here*
In *Casey*, this Court, in holding that a state cannot constitutionally proscribe abortion in all cases, reiterated that the Constitution protects a sphere of autonomy in which individuals must be permitted to make certain decisions for themselves. The Court began its analysis by pointing out that "[a]t the heart of liberty is the right to define one's own concept of existence, of meaning, of the universe, and of the mystery of human life." 505 U.S. at 851. Choices flowing out of these conceptions, on matters "involving the most intimate and personal choices a person may make in a lifetime, choices central to personal dignity and autonomy, are central to the liberty protected by the Fourteenth Amendment." *Id.* "Beliefs about these matters," the Court continued, "could not define the attributes of personhood were they formed under compulsion of the State." *Id.*
In language pertinent to the liberty interest asserted here, the Court explained why decisions about abortion fall within this category of "personal and intimate" decisions. A decision whether or not to have an abortion, "originat[ing] within the zone of conscience and belief," involves conduct in which "the liberty of the woman is at stake in a sense unique to the human condition and so unique to the law." *Id.* at 852. As such, the decision necessarily involves the very "destiny of the woman" and is inevitably "shaped to a large extent on her own conception of her spiritual imperatives and her place in society." *Id.* Precisely because of these characteristics of the decision, "the State is [not] entitled to proscribe [abortion] in all instances." Id. Rather, to allow a total prohibition on abortion would be to permit a state to impose one conception of the meaning and value of human existence on all individuals. This the Constitution forbids.
The Solicitor General nevertheless argues that the right to abortion could be supported on grounds other than this autonomy principle, grounds that would not apply here. He argues, for example, that the abortion right might flow from the great burden an unwanted child imposes on its mother's life. Brief for the United States at 14–15. But whether or not abortion rights could be defended on such grounds, they were not the grounds on which this Court in fact relied. To the contrary, the Court explained at length that the right flows from the constitutional protection accorded all individuals to "define one's own concept of existence, of

meaning, of the universe, and of the mystery of human life." *Casey*, 505 U.S. at 851.

The analysis in *Casey* compels the conclusion that the patient-plaintiffs have a liberty interest in this case that a state cannot burden with a blanket prohibition. Like a woman's decision whether to have an abortion, a decision to die involves one's very "destiny" and inevitably will be "shaped to a large extent on [one's] own conception of [one's] spiritual imperatives and [one's] place in society." *Id.* at 852. Just as a blanket prohibition on abortion would involve the improper imposition of one conception of the meaning and value of human existence on all individuals, so too would a blanket prohibition on assisted suicide. The liberty interest asserted here cannot be rejected without undermining the rationale of *Casey*. Indeed, the lower court opinions in the Washington case expressly recognized the parallel between the liberty interest in *Casey* and the interest asserted here. *See Compassion in Dying* v. *Washington*, 79 F.3d 790, 801 (9th Cir. 1996) (en banc) ("In deciding right-to-die cases, we are guided by the Court's approach to the abortion cases. *Casey* in particular provides a powerful precedent, for in that case the Court had the opportunity to evaluate its past decisions and to determine whether to adhere to its original judgment."), *aff'g*, 850 F. Supp. 1454, 1459 (W.D. Wash. 1994) ("[T]he reasoning in *Casey* [is] highly instructive and almost prescriptive . . ."). This Court should do the same.

B. Cruzan *Supports the Liberty Interest Asserted Here*

We agree with the Solicitor General that this Court's decision in *Cruzan . . .* supports the conclusion that a liberty interest is at stake in this case." Brief for the United States at 8. Petitioners, however, insist that the present cases can be distinguished because the right at issue in *Cruzan* was limited to a right to reject an unwanted invasion of one's body.[2] But this Court repeatedly has held that in appropriate circumstances a state may require individuals to accept unwanted invasions of the body. *See, e.g., Schmerber* v. *California*, 384 U.S. 757 (1966) (extraction of blood sample from individual suspected of driving while intoxicated, notwithstanding defendant's objection, does not violate privilege against self-incrimination or other constitutional rights); *Jacobson* v. *Massachusetts*, 197 U.S. 11 (1905) (upholding compulsory vaccination for smallpox as reasonable regulation for protection of public health).

There has been no suggestion that states are incapable of addressing [the dangers posed by physician-assisted suicide] through regulation.

The liberty interest at stake in *Cruzan* was a more profound one. If a competent patient has a constitutional right to refuse life-sustaining treatment, then, the Court implied, the state could not override that right. The regulations upheld in *Cruzan* were designed only to ensure that the individual's wishes were ascertained correctly. Thus, if *Cruzan* implies a right of competent patients to refuse life-sustaining treatment, that implication must be understood as resting not simply on a right to refuse bodily invasions but on the more profound right to refuse medical intervention when what is at stake is a momentous personal decision, such as the timing and manner of one's death. In her concurrence, Justice Sandra Day O'Connor expressly recognized that the right at issue involved a "deeply personal decision" that is "inextricably intertwined" with our notion of "self-determination." 497 U.S. at 287–89.

Cruzan also supports the proposition that a state may not burden a terminally ill patient's liberty interest in determining the time and manner of his death by prohibiting doctors from terminating life support. Seeking to distinguish *Cruzan*, Petitioners insist that a state may nevertheless burden that right in a different way by forbidding doctors to assist in the suicide of patients who are not on life-support machinery. They argue that doctors who remove life support are only allowing a natural process to end in death whereas doctors who prescribe lethal drugs are intervening to cause death. So, according to this argument, a state has an independent justification for forbidding doctors to assist in suicide that it does not have for forbidding them to remove life support. In the former case though not the latter, it is said, the state forbids an act of killing that is morally much more problematic than merely letting a patient die.

Several very detailed schemes for regulating physician-assisted suicide have been submitted.

This argument is based on a misunderstanding of the pertinent moral principles. It is certainly true that when a patient does not wish to die, different acts, each of which foreseeably results in his death, nevertheless have very different moral status. When several patients need organ transplants and organs are scarce, for example, it is morally permissible for a doctor to deny an organ to one patient, even though he will die without it, in order to give it to another. But it is certainly not permissible for a doctor to kill one patient in order to use his organs to save another. The morally significant difference between those two acts is not, however, that killing is a positive act and not providing an organ is a mere omission, or that killing someone is worse than merely allowing a "natural" process to result in death. It would be equally impermissible for a doctor to let an injured patient bleed to death, or to refuse antibiotics to a patient with pneumonia—in each case the doctor would have allowed death to result from a "natural" process—in order to make his organs available for transplant to others. A doctor violates his patient's rights whether the doctor acts or refrains from acting, against the patient's wishes, in a way that is designed to cause death.

When a competent patient does want to die, the moral situation is obviously different, because then it makes no sense to appeal to the patient's right not to be killed as a reason why an act designed to cause his death is impermissible. From the patient's point of view, there is no morally pertinent difference between a doctor's terminating treatment that keeps him alive, if that is what he wishes, and a doctor's helping him to end his own life by providing lethal pills he may take himself, when ready, if that is what he wishes—except that the latter may be quicker and more humane. Nor is that a pertinent difference from the doctor's point of view. If and when it is permissible for him to act with death in view, it does not matter which of those two means he and his patient choose. If it is permissible for a doctor deliberately to withdraw medical treatment in order to allow death to result from a natural process, then it is equally permissible for him to help his patient hasten his own death more actively, if that is the patient's express wish.

It is true that some doctors asked to terminate life support are reluctant and do so only in deference to a patient's right to compel them to remove unwanted invasions of his body. But other doctors, who believe that their most fundamental professional duty is to act in the patient's interests and that, in certain circumstances, it is in their patient's best interests to die, participate willingly in such decisions: they terminate life support to cause death because they know that is what their patient wants. *Cruzan* implied that a state may not absolutely prohibit a doctor from deliberately causing death, at the patient's request, in that way and for that reason. If so, then a state may not prohibit doctors from deliberately using more direct and often more humane means to the same end when that is what a patient prefers. The fact that failing to provide life-sustaining treatment may be regarded as "only letting nature take its course" is no more morally significant in this context, when the patient wishes to die, than in the other, when he wishes to live. Whether a doctor turns off a respirator in accordance with the patient's request or prescribes pills that a patient may take when he is ready to kill himself, the doctor acts with the same intention: to help the patient die.

The two situations do differ in one important respect. Since patients have a right not to have life-support machinery attached to their bodies, they have, in principle, a right to compel its removal. But that is not true in the case of assisted suicide: patients in certain circumstances have a right that the state not forbid doctors to assist in their deaths, but they have no right to compel a doctor to assist them. The right in question, that is, is only a right to the help of a willing doctor.

III. State Interests Do Not Justify a Categorical Prohibition on All Assisted Suicide

The Solicitor General concedes that "a competent, terminally ill adult has a constitutionally cognizable liberty interest in avoiding the kind of suffering experienced by the plaintiffs in this case." Brief for the United States at 8. He agrees that this interest extends not only to avoiding pain, but to avoiding an existence the patient believes to be one of intolerable indignity or incapacity as well. *Id.* at 12. The Solicitor General argues, however, that states nevertheless have the right to "override" this liberty interest altogether, because a state could reasonably conclude that allowing doctors to assist in suicide, even under the most stringent regulations and procedures that could be devised, would unreasonably endanger the lives of a number of patients who might ask for death in circumstances when it is plainly not in their interests to die or when their consent has been improperly obtained.

This argument is unpersuasive, however, for at least three reasons. *First,* in *Cruzan,* this Court noted that its various decisions supported the recognition of a general liberty interest in refusing medical treatment, even when such refusal could result in death. 497 U.S. at 278–79. The various risks described by the Solicitor General apply equally to those situations. For instance, a patient kept alive only by an elaborate and disabling life-support system might well become depressed, and doctors might be equally uncertain whether the depression is curable: such a patient might decide for death only because he has been advised that he will die soon anyway or that he will never live free of the burdensome apparatus, and either diagnosis might conceivably be mistaken. Relatives or doctors might subtly or crudely influence that decision, and state provision for the decision may (to the same degree in this case as if it allowed assisted suicide) be thought to encourage it.

The Constitution does not allow a state to deny patients a great variety of important choices.

Yet there has been no suggestion that states are incapable of addressing such dangers through regulation. In fact, quite the opposite is true. In *McKay* v. *Bergstedt*, 106 Nev. 808, 801 P.2d 617 (1990), for example, the Nevada Supreme Court held that "competent adult patients desiring to refuse or discontinue medical treatment" must be examined by two nonattending physicians to determine whether the patient is mentally competent, understands his prognosis and treatment options, and appears free of coercion or pressure in making his decision. *Id.* at 827–28, 801 P.2d at 630. See also: *id.* (in the case of terminally ill patients with natural life expectancy of less than six months, [a] patient's right of self-determination shall be deemed to prevail over state interests, whereas [a] non-terminal patient's decision to terminate life-support systems must first be weighed against relevant state interests by trial judge); [and] *In re Farrell*, 108 N.J. 335, 354, 529 A.2d 404, 413 (1987) ([which held that a] terminally ill patient requesting termination of life support must be determined to be competent and properly informed about [his] prognosis, available treatment options and risks, and to have made decision voluntarily and without coercion). Those protocols served to guard against precisely the dangers that the Solicitor General raises. The case law contains no suggestion that such protocols are inevitably insufficient to prevent deaths that should have been prevented.

Indeed, the risks of mistake are overall greater in the case of terminating life support. *Cruzan* implied that a state must allow individuals to make such decisions through an advance directive stipulating either that life support be terminated (or not initiated) in described circumstances when the individual was no longer competent to make such a decision himself, or that a designated proxy be allowed to make that decision. All the risks just described are present when the decision is made through or pursuant to such an advance directive, and a grave further risk is added: that the directive, though still in force, no longer represents the wishes of the patient. The patient might have changed his mind before he became incompetent, though he did not change the directive, or his proxy may make a decision that the patient would not have made himself if still competent. In *Cruzan*, this Court held that a state may limit these risks through reasonable regulation. It did not hold—or even suggest—that a state may avoid them through a blanket prohibition that, in effect, denies the liberty interest altogether.

Second, nothing in the record supports the [Solicitor General's] conclusion that no system of rules and regulations could adequately reduce the risk of mistake. As discussed above, the experience of states in adjudicating requests to have life-sustaining treatment removed indicates the opposite.[3] The Solicitor General has provided no persuasive reason why the same sort of procedures could not be applied effectively in the case of a competent individual's request for physician-assisted suicide.

Indeed, several very detailed schemes for regulating physician-assisted suicide have been submitted to the voters of some states[4] and one has been enacted.[5] In addition, concerned groups, including a group of distinguished professors of law and other professionals, have drafted and defended such schemes. *See, e.g.*, Charles H. Baron, et. al., *A Model State Act to Authorize and Regulate Physician-Assisted Suicide*, 33 Harv. J. Legis. 1 (1996). Such draft statutes propose a variety of protections and review procedures designed to insure against mistakes, and neither Washington nor New York attempted to show that such schemes would be porous or ineffective. Nor does the Solicitor General's brief: it relies instead mainly on flat and conclusory statements. It cites a New York Task Force report, written before the proposals just described were drafted, whose findings have been widely disputed and were implicitly rejected in the opinion of the Second Circuit below. *See generally Quill* v. *Vacco*, 80 F.3d 716 (2d Cir. 1996). The weakness of the Solicitor General's argument is signaled by his strong reliance on the experience in the Netherlands which, in effect, allows assisted suicide pursuant to published guidelines. Brief for the United States at 23–24. The Dutch guidelines are more permissive than the proposed and model American statutes, however. The Solicitor General deems the Dutch practice of ending the lives of people like neonates who cannot consent particularly noteworthy, for example, but that practice could easily and effectively be made illegal by any state regulatory scheme without violating the Constitution.

The Solicitor General's argument would perhaps have more force if the question before the Court were simply whether a state has any rational basis for an absolute prohibition; if that were the question, then it might be enough to call attention to risks a state might well deem not worth running. But as the Solicitor General concedes, the question here is a very different one: whether a state has interests sufficiently compelling to allow it to take the extraordinary step of altogether refusing the exercise of a liberty interest of constitutional dimension. In those circumstances, the burden is plainly on the state to demonstrate that the risk of mistakes is very high, and that no alternative to complete prohibition would adequately and effectively reduce those risks. Neither of the Petitioners has made such a showing.

Nor could they. The burden of proof on any state attempting to show this would be very high. Consider, for example, the burden a state would have to meet to show that it was entitled altogether to ban public speeches in favor of unpopular causes because it could not guarantee, either by regulations short of an outright ban or by increased police protection, that such speeches would not provoke a riot that would result in serious injury or death to an innocent party. Or that it was entitled to deny those accused of crime the procedural rights that the Constitution guarantees, such as the right to a jury trial, because the security risk those rights would impose on the community would be too great. One can posit extreme circumstances in which some such argument would succeed. *See, e.g., Korematsu v. United States,* 323 U.S. 214 (1944) (permitting United States to detain individuals of Japanese ancestry during wartime). But these circumstances would be extreme indeed, and the *Korematsu* ruling has been widely and severely criticized.

Third, it is doubtful whether the risks the Solicitor General cites are even of the right character to serve as justification for an absolute prohibition on the exercise of an important liberty interest. The risks fall into two groups. The first is the risk of medical mistake, including a misdiagnosis of competence or terminal illness. To be sure, no scheme of regulation, no matter how rigorous, can altogether guarantee that medical mistakes will not be made. But the Constitution does not allow a state to deny patients a great variety of important choices, for which informed consent is properly deemed necessary, just because the information on which the consent is given may, in spite of the most strenuous efforts to avoid mistake, be wrong. Again, these identical risks are present in decisions to terminate life support, yet they do not justify an absolute prohibition on the exercise of the right.

Patients have a crucial liberty interest in deciding for themselves.

The second group consists of risks that a patient will be unduly influenced by considerations that the state might deem it not in his best interests to be swayed by, for example, the feelings and views of close family members. Brief for the United States at 20. But what a patient regards as proper grounds for such a decision normally reflects exactly the judgments of personal ethics—of why his life is important and what affects its value—that patients have a crucial liberty interest in deciding for themselves. Even people who are dying have a right to hear and, if they wish, act on what others might wish to tell or suggest or even hint to them, and it would be dangerous to suppose that a state may prevent this on the ground that it knows better than its citizens when they should be moved by or yield to particular advice or suggestion in the exercise of their right to make fateful personal decisions for themselves. It is not a good reply that some people may not decide as they really wish—as they would decide, for example, if free from the "pressure" of others. That possibility could hardly justify the most serious pressure of all—the criminal law which tells them that they may not decide for death if they need the help of a doctor in dying, no matter how firmly they wish it.

There is a fundamental infirmity in the Solicitor General's argument. He asserts that a state may reasonably judge that the risk of "mistake" to some persons justifies a prohibition that not only risks but insures and even aims at what would undoubtedly be a vastly greater number of "mistakes" of the opposite kind—preventing many thousands of competent people who think that it disfigures their lives to continue living, in the only way left to them, from escaping that—to them—terrible injury. A state grievously and irreversibly harms such people when it prohibits that escape. The Solicitor General's argument may seem plausible to those who do not agree that individuals are harmed by being forced to live on in pain and what they regard as indignity. But many other people plainly do think that such individuals are harmed, and a state may not take one side in that essentially ethical or religious controversy as its justification for denying a crucial liberty.

Of course, a state has important interests that justify regulating physician-assisted suicide. It may be legitimate for a state to deny an opportunity for assisted suicide when it acts in what it reasonably judges to be the best interests of the potential suicide, and when its judgment on that issue does not rest on contested judgments about "matters involving the most intimate and personal choices a person may make in a lifetime, choices central to personal dignity and autonomy." *Casey*, 505 U.S. at 851. A state might assert, for example, that people who are not terminally ill, but who have formed a desire to die, are, as a group, very likely later to be grateful if they are prevented from taking their own lives. It might then claim that it is legitimate, out of concern for such people, to deny any of them a doctor's assistance [in taking their own lives].

This Court need not decide now the extent to which such paternalistic interests might override an individual's liberty interest. No one can plausibly claim, however—and it is noteworthy that neither Petitioners nor the Solicitor General does claim—that any such prohibition could serve the interests of any significant number of terminally ill patients. On the contrary, any paternalistic justification for an absolute prohibition of assistance to such patients would of necessity appeal to a widely contested religious or ethical conviction many of them, including the patient-plaintiffs, reject. Allowing *that* justification to prevail would vitiate the liberty interest.

Even in the case of terminally ill patients, a state has a right to take all reasonable measures to insure that a patient requesting such assistance has made an informed, competent, stable and uncoerced decision. It is plainly legitimate for a state to establish procedures through which professional and administrative judgments can be made about these matters, and to forbid doctors to assist in suicide when its reasonable procedures have not been satisfied. States may be permitted considerable leeway in designing such procedures. They may be permitted, within reason, to err on what they take to be the side of caution. But they may not use the bare possibility of error as justification for refusing to establish any procedures at all and relying instead on a flat prohibition.

Conclusion

Each individual has a right to make the "most intimate and personal choices central to personal dignity and autonomy." That right encompasses the right to exercise some control over the time and manner of one's death.

The patient-plaintiffs in these cases were all mentally competent individuals in the final phase of terminal illness and died within months of filing their claims.

Jane Doe described how her advanced cancer made even the most basic bodily functions such as swallowing, coughing, and yawning extremely painful and that it was "not possible for [her] to reduce [her] pain to an acceptable level of comfort and to retain an alert state." Faced with such circumstances, she sought to be able to "discuss freely with [her] treating physician [her] intention of hastening [her] death through the consumption of drugs prescribed for that purpose." *Quill* v. *Vacco*, 80 F.2d 716, 720 (2d Cir. 1996) (quoting declaration of Jane Doe).

George A. Kingsley, in advanced stages of AIDS which included, among other hardships, the attachment of a tube to an artery in his chest which made even routine functions burdensome and the development of lesions on his brain, sought advice from his doctors regarding prescriptions which could hasten his impending death. *Id.*

Jane Roe, suffering from cancer since 1988, had been almost completely bedridden since 1993 and experienced constant pain which could not be alleviated by medication. After undergoing counseling for herself and her family, she desired to hasten her death by taking prescription drugs. *Compassion in Dying* v. *Washington*, 850 F. Supp. 1454, 1456 (1994).

A state may not deny the liberty claimed by the patient-plaintiffs in these cases without providing them an opportunity to demonstrate . . . that the conviction they expressed for an early death is competent.

John Doe, who had experienced numerous AIDS-related ailments since 1991, was "especially cognizant of the suffering imposed by a lingering terminal illness because he was the primary caregiver for his long-term companion who died of AIDS" and sought prescription drugs from his physician to hasten his own death after entering the terminal phase of AIDS. *Id.* at 1456–57.

James Poe suffered from emphysema which caused him "a constant sensation of suffocating" as well as a cardiac condition which caused severe leg pain. Connected to an oxygen tank at all times but unable to calm the panic reaction associated with his feeling of suffocation even with regular doses of morphine, Mr. Poe sought physician-assisted suicide. *Id.* at 1457.

A state may not deny the liberty claimed by the patient-plaintiffs in these cases without providing them an opportunity to demonstrate, in whatever way the state might reasonably think wise and necessary, that the conviction they expressed for an early death is competent, rational, informed, stable, and uncoerced.

Affirming the decisions by the Courts of Appeals would establish nothing more than that there is such a constitutionally protected right in principle. It would establish only that some individuals, whose decisions for suicide plainly cannot be dismissed as irrational or foolish or premature, must be accorded a reasonable opportunity to show that their decision for death is informed and free. It is not necessary to decide precisely which patients are entitled to that opportunity. If, on the other hand, this Court reverses the decisions below, its decision could only be justified by the momentous proposition—a proposition flatly in conflict with the spirit and letter of the Court's past decisions—that an American citizen does not, after all, have the right, even in principle, to live and die in the light of his own religious and ethical beliefs, his own convictions about why his life is valuable and where its value lies.

Notes for Part I

1. *State of Washington et al.* v. *Glucksberg et al.* and *Vacco et al.* v. *Quill et al.*, argued January 8, 1997.

2. Though academic philosophers have been parties to amicus briefs before, as members of organizations or as representing an applied specialty like bioethics, I am unaware of any other occasion on which a group has intervened in Supreme Court litigation solely as general moral philosophers. All the signers to the brief contributed actively to its preparation, though we differ among ourselves about general issues of political philosophy and justice, and may have somewhat different opinions about how states might properly regulate assisted suicide if the principles the brief supports were recognized. We were wonderfully represented, both with the substance of the brief and the administration of its filing, by the Washington and New York law firm of Arnold & Porter, which donated its services and itself bore the considerable printing and administrative expenses. (Anand Agneshwar, Philip H. Curtis, Abe Krash, Janet Meissner Pritchard, Kent A. Yalowitz, and Peter L. Zimroth of that firm were particularly helpful.)

3. The voters of Oregon approved an assisted suicide scheme by referendum in 1994. A federal court held the scheme unconstitutional, but that decision is under appeal. [In October 1997, the Supreme Court upheld the Oregon law. And in November 1997 Oregon voters elected to retain the law.] The Netherlands has allowed assisted suicide, in practice, for several years, and there was much disagreement in the various briefs filed in these cases about the lessons to be drawn from the Dutch experience. The Northern Territories of Australia recently adopted legislation legalizing assisted suicide, but legislation to annul that legislation may be introduced in the Australian national Parliament. Switzerland also allows doctor-assisted suicide in highly restricted circumstances. See Seth Mydans, "Legal Euthanasia: Australia Faces a Grim Reality," *The New York Times*, February 2, 1997.

4. I described the circuit court decisions in an earlier article, "Sex and Death in the Courts," *The New York Review*, August 8, 1996.

5. Anthony L. Back et al., "Physician-Assisted Suicide and Euthanasia in Washington State," *Journal of the American Medical Association*, Volume 275, No. 42, pp. 919, 920, 922 (1996).

6. See David J. Doukas et al., "Attitudes and Behaviors on Physician Assisted Death: A Study of Michigan Oncologists," *Clinical Oncology*, Volume 13, p. 1055 (1995), and L. Slome et al., "Attitudes Toward Assisted Suicide in AIDS: A Five Year Comparison Study," conference abstract now available on the World Wide Web (1996) The amicus brief of the Association of Law School Professors offers other statistics to the same effect taken from other states and from nurses.

7. According to one respondent's brief, "Despite some imprecision in the empirical evidence, it has been estimated that between 5 percent and 52

percent of dying patients entering home palliative care units have been terminally sedated." The brief cites Paul Rousseau, "Terminal Sedation In The Care of Dying Patients," *Archives of Internal Medicine,* Volume 156, p. 1785 (1996).

8. The amicus brief of the Coalition of Hospice Professionals raised a frightening question about terminal sedation. "Unfortunately, while a terminally sedated patient exhibits an outwardly peaceful appearance, medical science cannot verify that the individual ceases to experience pain and suffering. To the contrary, studies of individuals who have been anaesthetized (with the same kinds of drugs used in terminal sedation) for surgery (and who are in a deeper comatose state than terminally sedated patients since their breathing must be sustained by a respirator) have demonstrated that painful stimuli applied to the patient will cause a significant increase in brain activity, even though there is no external physical response." See, e.g., Orlando R. Hung et al., "Thiopental Pharmacodynamics: Quantitation of Clinical and Electroencephalographic Depth of Anesthesia," *Anesthesiology,* Volume 77, p. 237 (1992).

9. *BANEC-Generated Guidelines for Comprehensive Care of the Terminally Ill.* Bay Area Network of Ethics Committees, September 1996.

10. Justice Antonin Scalia, who may also favor the first strategy, then suggested that "[P]roclaiming a liberty interest is cost-free so long as you can proclaim them and then say, however, they can be outweighed by various social policies adopted by the states. We can say there's a liberty interest in murdering people. . . ."

11. See my book *Freedom's Law* (Harvard University Press, 1996), pp. 29–31.

Notes for Part II

1. In *Cohen* v. *California,* 403 U.S. 15, 24 (1971), for example, this Court held that the First Amendment guarantee of free speech and expression derives from "the belief that no other approach would comport with the premise of individual dignity and choice upon which our political system rests." Interpreting the religion clauses of the First Amendment, this Court has explained that "[t]he victory for freedom of thought recorded in our Bill of Rights recognizes that in the domain of conscience there is a moral power higher than the State." *Girouard* v. *United States,* 328 U.S. 61, 68 (1946). And, in a number of Due Process cases, this Court has protected this conception of autonomy by carving out a sphere of personal family life that is immune from government intrusion. See, e.g., *Cleveland Bd. of Educ.* v. *LeFleur* 414 U.S. 632, 639 (1974) ("This Court has long recognized that freedom of personal choice in matters of marriage and family life is one of the liberties protected by the Due Process Clause of the Fourteenth Amendment."), *Eisenstadt* v. *Baird,* 405 U.S. 438, 453 (1973) (recognizing right "to be free from unwarranted governmental intrusion into matters so fundamentally affecting a person as the decision to bear and beget a child"); *Skinner* v. *Oklahoma,* 316 U.S. 535, 541(1942) (holding unconstitutional a state statute requiring the sterilization of individuals convicted of three offenses, in large part because the state's actions unwarrantedly intruded on marriage and procreation, "one of the basic civil rights of man"); *Loving* v. *Virginia,* 388 U.S. 1, 12 (1967) (striking down the criminal prohibition of interracial marriages as an infringement of the right to marry and holding that "[t]he freedom to marry has

long been recognized as one of the vital personal rights essential to the orderly pursuit of happiness by free men").

These decisions recognize as constitutionally immune from state intrusion that realm in which individuals make "intimate and personal" decisions that define the very character of their lives. See Charles Fried, *Right and Wrong* 146-47 (1978) ("What a person is, what he wants, the determination of his life plan, of his concept of the good, are the most intimate expressions of self-determination, and by asserting a person's responsibility for the results of this self-determination, we give substance to the concept of liberty.").

2. In that case, the parents of Nancy Cruzan, a woman who was in a persistent vegetative state following an automobile accident, asked the Missouri courts to authorize doctors to end life support and therefore her life. The Supreme Court held that Missouri was entitled to demand explicit evidence that Ms. Cruzan had made a decision that she would not wish to be kept alive in those circumstances, and to reject the evidence the family had offered as inadequate. But a majority of justices assumed, for the sake of the argument, that a competent patient has a right to reject life-preserving treatment, and it is now widely assumed that the Court would so rule in an appropriate case.

3. When state protocols are observed, sometimes the patient is permitted to die and sometimes not. *See, e.g., In re Tavel,* 661 A.2d 1061 (Del. 1995) (affirming finding that petitioner-daughter had proven by clear and convincing evidence that incompetent patient would want life-support systems removed); *In re Martin,* 450 Mich. 204, 538 N.W.2d 399 (1995) (holding that wife's testimony and affidavit did not constitute clear and convincing evidence of incompetent patient's pre-injury decision to decline life-sustaining medical treatment in patient's present circumstances); *DiGrella v. Elston,* 858 S.W.2d 698,710 (Ky. 1993) ("If the attending physician, the hospital or nursing home ethics committee where the patient resides, and the legal guardian or next of kin all agree and document the patient's wishes and condition, and if no one disputes their decision, no court order is required to proceed to carry out [an incompetent] patient's wishes"); *Mack v. Mack,* 329 Md. 188, 618 A.2d 744 (1993) (holding that wife failed to provide clear and convincing evidence that incompetent husband would want life support removed) *In re Doe,* 411 Mass. 512, 583 N.E.2d 1263 (applying doctrine of substituted judgment and holding that evidence supported finding that, if incompetent patient were capable of making a choice, she would remove life support).

4. For example, 46 percent of California voters supported Proposition 161, which would have legalized physician-assisted suicide, in November 1992. The measure was a proposed amendment to Cal. Penal Code § 401 (1992) which currently makes assisted suicide a felony. Those who did not vote for the measure cited mainly religious reasons or concerns that the proposed law was flawed because it lacked safeguards against abuse and needed more restrictions that might be easily added, such as a waiting period and a psychological examination. Alison C. Hall, *To Die with Dignity: Comparing Physician-Assisted Suicide in the United States, Japan, and the Netherlands,* 74 Wash. U.L.Q. 803, 817 n.84 (1996).

5. In November 1994, Oregon voters approved the Oregon Death with Dignity Act through voter initiative, legalizing physician-assisted suicide un-

der limited circumstances. Oregon Death with Dignity Act, Or. Rev. Stat. §§ 127.800–.827 (1995). Under the Oregon Act, a capable adult resident of the state, who

> has been determined by the attending physician and consulting physician to be suffering from a terminal disease, and who has voluntarily expressed his or her wish to die, may make a written request for medication for the purpose of ending his life in a humane and dignified manner in accordance with [the provisions of the Act].

Or. Rev. Stat. § 127.805 (1995). The Act provides specific definitions of essential terms such as "incapable" and "terminal disease." The Act also provides numerous other regulations designed to safeguard the integrity of the process.

7

Physician-Assisted Suicide Is Not a Constitutional Right

Carl H. Coleman and Tracy E. Miller

Carl H. Coleman is acting executive director of the New York State Task Force on Life and the Law in New York City. Tracy E. Miller is visiting scholar for law and health policy in the Department of Health Policy at Mount Sinai School of Medicine in New York City.

Historically, federal and state courts have made a distinction between the right to refuse medical treatment and physician-assisted suicide. While they have generally upheld the constitutionality of the right to refuse treatment, they have not found similar constitutional support for the right to assisted suicide. State laws against assisted suicide are justified in order to protect individual liberties. Legalized physician-assisted suicide would pose a significant threat to weak and easily influenced patients who might be coerced by their physicians or family members into the decision to end their lives. The courts must protect the interests of these vulnerable individuals by rejecting claims that physician-assisted suicide is a constitutional right.

Editor's note: In June 1997, the Supreme Court ruled on two cases in which state laws against physician-assisted suicide were challenged as unconstitutional. The Court upheld the laws, effectively refusing to grant Americans a constitutional right to physician-assisted suicide.

On November 8, 1994, Oregon became the first state in the nation to legalize assisted suicide. Passage of Proposition 16 was a milestone in the campaign to make assisted suicide a legal option. The culmination of years of effort, the Oregon vote followed on the heels of failed referenda in California and Washington, and other unsuccessful attempts to enact state laws guaranteeing the right to suicide assistance. Indeed, in 1993, four states passed laws strengthening or clarifying their ban against assisted suicide.[1] No doubt, Proposition 16 is likely to renew the effort to legalize assisted suicide at the state level.

From Carl H. Coleman and Tracy E. Miller, "Stemming the Tide: Assisted Suicide and the Constitution," *Journal of Law, Medicine, and Ethics*, vol. 23 (1995), pp. 389–97. Reprinted with permission of the American Society of Law, Medicine, and Ethics.

The battle over assisted suicide is also unfolding in the courts. Litigation challenging Proposition 16 on the grounds that it violates the equal protection clause is ongoing in Oregon.[2] [The Oregon law was upheld by the Supreme Court in October 1997; in November 1997, Oregon voters chose to keep the law.] More significantly, three cases, two in federal courts and one in Michigan state court, have been brought to establish assisted suicide as a constitutionally protected right. These three cases have yielded important rulings that foreshadow the ultimate resolution of this issue by the United States Supreme Court. The federal lawsuit challenging Washington State's law barring assisted suicide as unconstitutional, *Compassion in Dying v. State of Washington*, resulted first in a much-publicized district court ruling striking down the law.[3] On March 9, 1995, the United States Court of Appeals for the Ninth Circuit overturned that decision, holding that a right to assisted suicide is not protected by the United States Constitution.[4] In a similar lawsuit challenging New York's laws prohibiting assisted suicide, *Quill v. Koppell*, the district court upheld the statutes, dismissing the lawsuit after a preliminary hearing.[5]

The Michigan Supreme Court decision was a consolidated ruling on four cases. Three cases, each identified as *People v. Kevorkian*, arose from charges brought against Jack Kevorkian for his role in the deaths of five patients. The fourth case, *Hobbins v. Attorney General*, was a civil suit brought by a terminally ill patient, one of her friends, and seven health care professionals who sought to strike down Michigan's statute barring assisted suicide as unconstitutional. On December 13, 1994, the Michigan court issued a consolidated ruling in the four cases, upholding the statute's constitutionality.[6] In *Kevorkian*, the court also found that the absence of a specific statute prohibiting assisted suicide at the time one of the cases arose does not preclude the common law charge of murder for suicide assistance where death is "the direct and natural result of a defendant's act."

The central question at stake in the ongoing litigation is whether the courts will override the historic distinction between withholding and withdrawing medical treatment and active assistance to commit suicide. The litigation has also posed more general questions about the scope of protected "liberty interests" under the Constitution, and the Supreme Court's willingness to apply principles established in cases involving human reproduction to other spheres of private activity.

The first part of this article analyzes the three cases on assisted suicide decided to date in light of relevant Supreme Court rulings, most notably the Court's holding in *Cruzan v. Director, Missouri Department of Health*.[7] It concludes that the Supreme Court is unlikely to hold that decisions about suicide implicate any constitutionally protected rights or liberty interests. The second part examines the state interests underlying laws against assisted suicide. Because such laws are supported by important state interests, they should be upheld as constitutional even if they limit individual autonomy in a particular case. [In June 1997, the Supreme Court ruled that state laws prohibiting physician-assisted suicide are constitutional.]

The Supreme Court has classified certain rights as "fundamental," and subjects laws infringing those rights to "strict scrutiny." A law will survive strict scrutiny only if it is justified by "compelling governmental interest[s]" and if it is "narrowly tailored" to achieve those interests.[8] The

Court has also recognized that certain other rights, while not rising to the status of a fundamental right, implicate constitutionally protected "liberty interests." Laws that infringe on these interests are subjected to a balancing test, under which a court must weigh the "individual's interest in liberty against the State's asserted reason for restraining individual liberty."[9] Laws that do not infringe on either fundamental rights or constitutionally protected liberty interests receive only minimal judicial scrutiny, and will be upheld as long as they are "rationally related" to a legitimate governmental goal.[10]

The right to decide about medical treatment has long been protected by the common law.[11] Over the past two decades, as treatments to preserve life have expanded, the courts have consistently affirmed that the right to decide about treatment extends to the refusal of treatment, even when death will result.[12] Federal and state courts have also found that the right to decide about treatment is protected under the Constitution. In 1990, in a case involving Nancy Cruzan, a young woman who had become permanently unconscious following a car accident, the Supreme Court recognized that "[t]he principle that a competent person has a constitutionally protected liberty interest in refusing unwanted medical treatment may be inferred from our prior decisions." This finding in *Cruzan* is at the heart of the litigation on assisted suicide. In constitutional terms, does assisted suicide implicate the same liberty interest as withdrawing or withholding of life-sustaining treatment? Specifically, does *Cruzan* protect a broad right to control the timing and manner of death, or does it stand for the more limited proposition that individuals have the right to be free of unwanted bodily intrusions?

Advocates of a constitutional right to assisted suicide contend that the individual's right to self-determination encompasses all decisions about the timing and manner of death. In their view, a right to assisted suicide is implicit in the right to refuse life-sustaining treatment, as both practices seek to give individuals "control over when they die, where they die, and their physical and mental state at the time of their death."[13] According to this position, distinctions between the refusal of treatment and suicide are artificial, because both practices stem from the individual's intent to end his/her life, and both require acts or omissions that directly cause the individual's death.[14] Rejecting the distinction between actively causing death through assisted suicide or euthanasia and passively allowing a patient to die by terminating treatment, advocates of a right to suicide emphasize that the law often equates omissions with deliberate acts.[15] Also central to their argument is an emphasis on the personal nature of the two decisions. As articulated by the district court in *Compassion in Dying,*

> [t]here is no more profoundly personal decision, nor one which is closer to the heart of personal liberty, than the choice which a terminally ill person makes to end his or her suffering and hasten an inevitable death. From a constitutional perspective, the court does not believe that a distinction can be drawn between refusing life-sustaining medical treatment and physician-assisted suicide by an uncoerced, mentally competent, terminally ill adult.[16]

Aside from the district court in *Compassion in Dying,* however, the courts have uniformly rejected the notion that refusal of treatment and assisted suicide raise equivalent constitutional concerns. In two decades of decisions affirming the constitutional right to refuse life-saving medical treatment, courts have carefully distinguished that right from a right to commit suicide, relying on differences in both intention and causation. These courts have reasoned that individuals who refuse unwanted medical treatment do not intend to cause death, but instead seek to allow their disease to take its natural course.[17] The opinions also suggest that, when treatment is refused, the ultimate cause of death is the underlying disease, not the patient's own decision or act.[18] Indeed, judicial precedents supporting the right to forgo treatment have expressly recognized that preventing suicide is a legitimate state interest.[19]

The Supreme Court is unlikely to hold that decisions about suicide implicate any constitutionally protected rights.

While the Supreme Court itself has never squarely addressed the constitutionality of laws against assisted suicide, its decision in *Cruzan* strongly supports the distinction between the right to refuse treatment and a more general right to control the timing and manner of death. In *Cruzan,* the Supreme Court noted that "the majority of states in this country have laws imposing criminal penalties on one who assists another to commit suicide,"[20] and it did not suggest that these laws might be constitutionally infirm. In addition, the Court expressly recognized the state's interest in protecting human life, asserting that a state need not "remain neutral in the face of an informed and voluntary decision by a physically able adult to starve to death." Perhaps most importantly, *Cruzan* relied heavily on cases recognizing the right to refuse physical intrusions, such as bodily searches and the forced administration of psychotropic medications. When read as a case about resisting unwanted intrusions, the applicability of *Cruzan* to decisions about assisted suicide is tenuous at best. Unlike the imposition of life-sustaining treatment against a patient's will, which requires a direct invasion of bodily integrity and, for some patients, the use of physical restraints, restrictions on assisted suicide do not entail physical intrusions. Rather, these laws prevent individuals from intervening in the natural process of dying. Finally, it is significant that only one justice in *Cruzan,* Justice Antonin Scalia, found that the right to withdraw treatment is equivalent to suicide, and he argued that neither practice merits constitutional protection. None of the justices who recognized a constitutional liberty interest in refusing life-sustaining treatment agreed that the refusal of treatment is tantamount to suicide as a matter of law.

The three recent decisions upholding the constitutionality of laws against assisted suicide all relied heavily on *Cruzan* in determining that the refusal of treatment and suicide involve fundamentally different constitutional concerns. While the district court in *Quill* offered little analysis of the issue, beyond stating that "suicide has a sufficiently different legal significance from requesting withdrawal of treatment so that a fundamental right to suicide cannot be implied from *Cruzan*,"[21] the Michigan Supreme Court and the Ninth Circuit addressed the distinction at length. In *Kevorkian*, the Michigan court stressed the difference between an affirmative act to end life and termination of a "contrived intervention" so that nature may take its course. The court drew an analogy to the difference in tort law between *misfeasance*, or active misconduct, and *nonfeasance*, or passive inaction, stating that the line between action and inaction is well established in the law. The Ninth Circuit, in reversing the district court's decision in *Compassion in Dying*, cited *Olmstead v. United States* for the proposition that the core of constitutionally protected privacy interests is the "right to be let alone."[22] Emphasizing that assisted suicide requires another person's affirmative participation, the court concluded that "[w]hen you assert a claim that another—and especially another licensed by the state—should help you bring about your death, you ask for more than being let alone; you ask that the state, in protecting its own interest, not prevent its licensee from killing. The difference is not of degree but of kind."[23]

Assisted suicide and the right to reproductive autonomy

The second prong of the argument for recognizing a constitutional right to assisted suicide rests on an analogy to the rights protected in the context of human reproduction and family life. The district court in *Compassion in Dying* relied extensively on this argument, suggesting that the Supreme Court's 1992 decision in *Planned Parenthood v. Casey*,[24] which reaffirmed the constitutional right to abortion, is "almost prescriptive" as applied to assisted suicide. Again emphasizing the personal nature of the choices at stake, the court concluded that, like a pregnant woman's decision to abort, "the decision of a terminally ill person to end his or her life involves the most intimate and personal choices a person may make in a lifetime." The court also found the two decisions comparable because the individual will suffer if the state precludes the option that the individual prefers. As stated by Judge Rothstein, "the suffering of a terminally ill person cannot be deemed any less intimate or personal, or any less deserving of protect from unwarranted government interference, than that of a pregnant woman."[25]

> *The Court expressly recognized the state's interest in protecting human life.*

This reliance on cases in the area of reproductive freedom, however, is difficult to reconcile with the Supreme Court's own narrow reading of those cases. As Alexander Capron has observed, "the Court has repeatedly made clear that the liberty enshrined in these cases relates solely to the decision to bear or beget children—even other forms of intimate sexual relations are not protected from state regulation by the recognized right to privacy."[26] Most notably, in its 1986 decision in *Bowers v. Hardwick*,[27] the Court found that the individual's interest in reproductive and sexual autonomy was not implicated by a Georgia statute that prohibited sodomy between consenting adults in their own homes. Focusing almost exclusively on the historical opposition to homosexual activity, the Court concluded that a right to "homosexual sodomy" is not "deeply rooted in this nation's history or in the concept of ordered liberty." Likewise, in *Michael H. v. Gerald D.*,[28] the Court rejected a constitutional challenge to a statute that prevented a natural father from asserting paternity over a child born to a woman who was married to another man. In reaching its conclusion, the Court specifically rejected the father's contention that precedents in the area of reproduction and family life stood for a broad constitutional interest in maintaining and developing family ties. Instead, the Court noted the lack of historical support for the narrow right to assert paternity rights for a child born out of an adulterous relationship, and it upheld the statute against constitutional attack.

While the merits of the Court's reliance on history as a means of constitutional analysis is open to question, its effect on the constitutional status of laws prohibiting assisted suicide is clear. In contrast to the right to refuse treatment, which has a well-established history in the laws of informed consent and battery, assisted suicide has long been banned in this country. At the time the Fourteenth Amendment was ratified, twenty-one of the thirty-seven existing states prohibited assisted suicide by statute or common law.[29] Currently, assisted suicide is a statutory offense in thirty-two states. In states without statutes prohibiting assisted suicide, persons who aid suicide may still be subject to prosecution for murder or manslaughter.[30] Indeed, suicide was illegal in many states for much of this nation's history, and, even after decriminalization, society continued to discourage it. As explained in the 1980 commentary to the Model Penal Code, the decriminalization of suicide did not reflect social approval of suicide as much as a recognition that punishment was an inappropriate response to a suicide attempt.[31]

Assisted suicide has long been banned in this country.

This historical opposition to suicide and the well-established legal support for the right to refuse treatment have carried considerable weight in the constitutional analysis to date. According to the Michigan Supreme Court in *Kevorkian*, which discussed the legal history of suicide and assisted suicide at length, "[i]t would be an impermissibly radical departure from existing tradition, and from the principles that underlie that tradition, to declare that there is such a fundamental right protected by the Due Process Clause."[32] The Ninth Circuit also emphasized the historical opposition to suicide and assisted suicide in its decision in *Compassion in Dying*. Criticizing the district court for its expansive reading of *Casey* and other decisions in the area of reproductive rights, the court commented that

> [t]o take three sentences out of an opinion over thirty pages in length dealing with the highly charged subject of abortion and to find these sentences 'almost prescriptive' in ruling on a statute proscribing the promotion of suicide is to make an enormous leap, to do violence to the context, and

to ignore the differences between the regulation of reproduction and the prevention of the promotion of killing a
patient at his or her request.[33]

History aside, the Supreme Court is unlikely to extend the constitutional right to privacy to decisions about suicide for the simple reason that
it has already refused to characterize the right to refuse life-sustaining
treatment as a fundamental privacy right. Prior to *Cruzan,* state and federal courts had found that the right to refuse treatment was protected as a
privacy right under the Constitution.[34] In *Cruzan,* however, the Court expressly rejected this analysis, stating that the "issue is more properly ana-
lyzed in terms of a Fourteenth Amendment liberty interest." Having already determined that the refusal of treatment—although deserving of
some constitutional protection—does not implicate the right to privacy established in cases dealing with reproduction and family life, the Court is
unlikely to conclude that *Casey* and other reproductive rights cases mandate recognition of assisted suicide as a fundamental constitutional right.

Should assisted suicide be established as a constitutional right?

As suggested by the analysis above, it is doubtful that the current
Supreme Court would find that assisted suicide implicates any constitutional rights or liberty interests. If this is correct, laws against assisted suicide would be subject to the same standard of review that applies to most
other forms of social and economic legislation; that standard asks only
whether a law is "rationally related" to a legitimate governmental goal.
Laws subjected to this rational relationship standard are almost invariably
upheld against constitutional attack.

It would be unfortunate, however, to rest the constitutionality of laws
against assisted suicide exclusively on this current Court's jurisprudence.
The Supreme Court has repeatedly proclaimed its unwillingness to "an-
nounc[e] rights not readily identifiable in the Constitution's text,"[35] placing history and tradition over individual autonomy in all but a few, narrowly defined circumstances. Yet, the constitutionality of laws against
assisted suicide need not be based on such a narrow conception of individual rights. While advocates of assisted suicide seek to portray such laws
as symbols of a state-imposed morality, unsympathetic to individual suffering, prohibitions on assisted suicide are in fact supported by important
state interests, all of which are fully consistent with recognition of individual autonomy as a vital constitutional concern.[36] These state interests
justify upholding the constitutionality of laws against assisted suicide,
even if it is conceded that such laws implicate individual liberty interests
and thus demand a heightened standard of judicial review.

Foremost among the state's interests is the prevention of assisted suicide when the decision to commit suicide does not reflect a rational, settled commitment to die, but results from mental illness or improperly
managed physical pain. Advocates of legalization concede this interest,
but argue that this description does not apply to a terminally ill person
who chooses to "hasten inevitable death" to avoid prolonged suffering.[37]
As studies have confirmed, however, the overwhelming majority of suici-

dal individuals—including those who are elderly and terminally ill—suffer from a treatable psychiatric disorder, most commonly depression, often accompanied by improperly managed physical pain.[38] In this respect, it is crucial to distinguish thoughts about suicide (suicidal ideation) from a genuine desire to take one's own life. Thinking about suicide can be an integral component of dealing with terminal illness, and can provide patients with a sense of control as they adjust to the reality of their disease. Genuine suicidal tendencies, however, are far less frequent, and generally correlate with clinical depression or improperly managed physical pain.[39]

Undertreatment of pain and depression are common in current clinical practice.

While the most vocal advocates for assisted suicide, including the patient-plaintiffs in the pending lawsuits, allege that they have received all available pain relief and that they are not depressed, most patients in this country are not so fortunate. Undertreatment of pain and depression are common in current clinical practice, despite the fact that pain and depression can be effectively treated in all but the rarest cases.[40] Most physicians are not adequately trained to diagnose depression, especially in complex cases where patients are terminally ill. Even if diagnosed, undertreatment for depression, particularly among the elderly, is pervasive.[41] Numerous barriers also contribute to the widespread inadequacy of pain relief and palliative care in current clinical practice, including a lack of professional knowledge and training, unjustified fears about physical and psychological dependence, poor pain assessment, pharmacy practices, and the reluctance of patients and their families to talk about pain or to seek relief.[42] The high correlation between suicide and untreated pain and depression, combined with the serious undertreatment of these conditions in current clinical practice, means that legalizing assisted suicide would lead to the deaths of many individuals whose requests for assistance result from inadequate medical care, not a rational, firm commitment to die.

The risk that individuals will seek suicide assistance due to depression, untreated pain, or other symptoms is likely to be most pronounced for the poor, minorities, and others without adequate access to health care. Studies have shown that members of minority groups are three times more likely than whites to receive inadequate therapy to relieve pain.[43] Other studies reveal strong disparities between minorities and others in access to basic medical care.[44] Those who are uninsured or covered by Medicaid may also face additional risks as managed care arrangements become more common, given the financial incentives under managed care to underutilize services or to limit access to care.[45] The state has a strong interest in protecting these vulnerable populations from the risks associated with legalizing assisted suicide, especially in a society that has consistently failed to guarantee access to adequate medical care.

The state's interest in prohibiting assisted suicide also derives from its responsibility for regulating the medical profession and for protecting patients, as consumers of health care, from physicians' biases and mistakes.

As the Ninth Circuit found in *Compassion in Dying,* physicians—even those acting with the best of motives—are likely to exercise considerable influence over a patient's decision to end his/her life. "For all medical treatments, physicians decide which patients are the candidates. If assisted suicide was acceptable professional practice, physicians would make a judgment as to who was a good candidate for it. Physician neutrality and patient autonomy, independent of their physician's advice, are largely myths. Most patients do what their doctors recommend."[46] Physicians' role in choosing "appropriate" candidates for assisted suicide would pose serious risks. Such decisions will inevitably be affected by physicians' own attitudes about illness, physical dependence, pain, and disability. According to a recent study, "burn-out" among health care professionals correlates strongly with the willingness to endorse assisted suicide.[47] In some cases, "offering assisted suicide and euthanasia may reflect physicians' own frustration in situations when medicine can provide care but not cure."[48] Given the state's responsibility for overseeing the medical profession, a legislative judgment that physicians lack the ability to distribute lethal medications without serious incidents of mistake and abuse should be entitled to considerable judicial deference.

Laws against assisted suicide are further justified by the state's interest in promoting compassionate treatment of the ill and disabled. If assisted suicide is legalized, the option may seem most appropriate for those whose care is least appealing—patients with AIDS or other illnesses that carry social stigmas, patients who pose a risk to health care providers, such as those with multidrug-resistant tuberculosis, or patients who are unwilling to comply with treatment as a result of mental illness or substance abuse. As Leon Kass asks, "[h]ow easily will [physicians] be able to care for patients when it is always possible to think of killing them as a 'therapeutic' option? . . . Physicians get tired of treating patients who are on their way down."[49] Recognizing this risk, the Ninth Circuit concluded that the state's interest in "protecting all of the handicapped from societal indifference and antipathy" supports prohibitions on assisted suicide, especially in light of society's "insidious bias against the handicapped . . . coupled with a cost-saving mentality."[50]

> *The state's interest in prohibiting assisted suicide . . . derives from its responsibility for . . . protecting patients.*

Advocates of legalization acknowledge many of these risks, but argue that the law must allow for exceptions, so that individuals who have received appropriate treatment for pain, depression, and other symptoms, yet still desire assisted suicide, can have their wishes carried out. It is highly unlikely, however, that a law with exceptions could be effectively implemented in current clinical practice. While advocates of legalization suggest that guidelines could be established to assist physicians in selecting appropriate candidates for assisted suicide, the guidelines proposed to date are premised on circumstances far removed from the reality that confronts most terminally ill patients today. For example, one prominent set of guidelines presumes the existence of a caring doctor-patient relationship, one in which the doctor explores all the medical options available, sorts out the reasons motivating the desire for suicide, and turns back at any sign of ambivalence by the patient.[51] Neither legislative fiat nor professional guidelines could establish this kind of relationship. Nor would the state have any effective mechanism to monitor the quality of doctor-patient discussions about suicide as an alternative to continued medical care.

If, as studies suggest, the number of people who want assisted suicide in the absence of depression or improperly managed physical pain is extremely small, and legalizing the practice for the sake of these few—whatever safeguards are written into the law—would endanger the lives of a far larger group of individuals, then laws prohibiting assisted suicide are a valid exercise of state legislative authority.[52] In other contexts, the Supreme Court has clearly affirmed that statutes are not unconstitutional simply because they apply to some cases where the state's interest is not directly implicated.[53] Even when fundamental rights are at stake, the Court has held that states need not make exceptions for individuals if such exceptions would "unduly interfere with fulfillment of the governmental interest."[54] These principles support state prohibitions on assisted suicide, even if it is conceded that such prohibitions interfere with individual liberty in some cases. In the words of Seth Kreimer, "[t]he State may grant that the prohibition imposes real and substantial costs on both patients who seek to end their lives and on their families, but may at the same time decide that it must impose those costs in the effort to avoid the premature death of others and to facilitate medical care that will preserve lives."[55]

> *It is highly unlikely . . . that a law with exceptions could be effectively implemented.*

Establishing a constitutional right to assisted suicide would be particularly dangerous because no doctrinal basis exists that could justify limiting the right to the terminally ill or other narrowly defined classes of individuals as a matter of constitutional law. Although the plaintiffs in the pending lawsuits limit their claims to the terminally ill, cases establishing the right to refuse life-sustaining medical treatment strongly suggest that line-drawing between the terminally ill and others who are suffering could not be maintained. As stated by the New Jersey Supreme Court in *Matter of Conroy,*[56] a case involving the refusal of treatment for a demented but not terminally ill woman, "a competent person's common law and constitutional rights do not depend on the quality or value of his life." Likewise, the New York Court of Appeals in *Fosmire v. Nicoleau*[57] rejected the patient's medical status as a constitutional benchmark, upholding the right of a physically healthy thirty-six-year-old pregnant woman to refuse blood transfusions following a cesarean section. As the Ninth Circuit observed in *Compassion in Dying,* "[t]he attempt to restrict such rights to the terminally ill is illusory. If such liberty exists in this context, . . . every man and woman in the United States must enjoy it."[58] Indeed, many cases of assisted suicide that have captured the public's attention have involved individuals with Alzheimer's disease, muscular dystrophy, or other nonterminal conditions. These individuals might have had years of life ahead of them had their requests for assistance not been granted.

The difficulty of setting parameters on the right to suicide assistance is compounded by the fact that the right is directly tied to notions of suffering. Suffering is an inherently subjective criterion that is not limited to physical illness but encompasses psychological pain as well. As one of the physicians who filed the lawsuit to strike down New York's ban on assisted suicide recently advocated, doctors considering suicide assistance must be allowed to take into account the patient's "psychological and spiritual suffering," not just physical symptoms.[59] This extension of assisted suicide to those who are psychologically suffering but not physically ill has already occurred in the Netherlands, where assisted suicide and euthanasia are legally sanctioned.[60] Similarly, any constitutional liberty interest grounded in the notion of a right to control the timing and manner of death could not logically be limited to assisted suicide, but would necessarily extend to direct steps, such as a physician-administered lethal injection, for patients who desire or need that option. As Lawrence Tribe has argued, the difficulty of limiting a right "to determine when and how to die" is the principal reason that courts have been reluctant to recognize such a right as a matter of constitutional law.[61]

Admittedly, allowing individuals to refuse life-sustaining treatment necessarily presents some of the same risks associated with assisted suicide, including the risk that patients will refuse treatment because of clinical depression or feelings that they burden family or caretakers. However, these risks are limited because the refusal of treatment causes death only for individuals whose continued existence requires extensive medical support. By contrast, if a right to assisted suicide were recognized, it would have no such built-in safeguard; even limits based on the patient's medical condition or life expectancy would be difficult to maintain as a matter of constitutional law. The right would necessarily extend to a broader, more elastic class of "suffering" individuals, thus greatly expanding the risks. Moreover, decisions to forgo life-sustaining treatment are often carried out in a hospital or another health care facility, which allows for quality assurance and oversight of the decision and the care provided. The prescription of lethal medication, by contrast, will occur most often in the privacy of a doctor's office or the patient's home, settings where effective oversight to minimize error or abuse would be more difficult, if not unrealizable.

Establishing a constitutional right to assisted suicide would be particularly dangerous.

Even more significantly, banning the refusal of life-sustaining treatment would impose a burden on individual liberty far more severe than any burden entailed by prohibiting assisted suicide. Unlike assisted suicide, the refusal of life-sustaining treatment is an integral dimension of medical practice; it is estimated that approximately 70 percent of all hospital and nursing home deaths follow the refusal of some form of medical intervention.[62] Prohibiting the refusal of treatment would therefore require the widespread restraint of patients unwilling to submit to invasive procedures at the end of their lives. Such a policy would be an abuse of medicine, placing patients at the mercy of every technological advance. In addition, such prohibitions might deter individuals from seeking medical treatment in the first place, thereby undermining society's interest in caring for the seriously ill. By contrast, prohibitions on assisted suicide only interfere with the individual liberty of those individuals whose requests for suicide assistance do not stem from depression or treatable physical pain. Because the vast majority of requests for suicide assistance do not come from such individuals, prohibitions on assisted suicide are far less intrusive than prohibitions on the refusal of life-sustaining medical treatment.

These distinctions between decisions to forgo life-sustaining treatment and to assist suicide provide a sound constitutional basis to distinguish between the two practices. They do not, however, require states to ban assisted suicide, nor do they preclude states from affirmatively legalizing the practice, provided that the standards and procedures adopted are not otherwise constitutionally infirm. Of particular relevance here are the requirements of equal protection and due process. Under the equal protection clause, a statute legalizing assisted suicide could not limit the persons eligible for assistance based on irrational or arbitrary grounds—for example, by allowing assisted suicide for persons with cancer but not for persons in the terminal phase of heart disease. Basic principles of due process would also prevent the imposition of any standard or procedure that is not "rationally related" to the statute's asserted goals.

Suffering is an inherently subjective criterion that is not limited to physical illness but encompasses psychological pain as well.

These issues were raised directly in *Lee v. Oregon*,[63] a federal district court ruling that struck down Oregon's recently enacted public referendum legalizing assisted suicide for the terminally ill. The plaintiffs in *Lee* had argued that the statute violated the equal protection clause by creating an arbitrary distinction between the terminally ill and others, denying the terminally ill the protection from inappropriate death accorded to other patients. The court agreed with this claim, although the opinion suggests that the court's real concern rested not with the distinction between the terminally ill and others, but with the inadequacy of the procedures designed to ensure that assisted suicide would be limited to terminally ill, competent individuals. For example, the court emphasized that the referendum does not require any psychiatric evaluation of candidates for assisted suicide, nor does it require the person to take the lethal medication at the time of the prescription or under the supervision of a physician. Most troubling to the court was the reliance on "good faith" as the standard for liability applied to physicians under the referendum, a standard that exempts physicians from liability if they act negligently in complying with any of the safeguards under the law. Contrasting this standard with the standard of "reasonable medical practice" that Oregon law imposes in other medical contexts, the court stated that "there is no set of facts under which it would be rational for terminally ill patients . . . to receive a standard of care from their physicians under which it did not matter whether they acted with reasonableness, according to professional standards."[64]

Such a dramatic change in law would pose serious risks for vulnerable individuals.

While we share the court's concerns about the wisdom of the Oregon referendum and the inadequacies of the procedures under the law, we believe that the opinion is likely to be reversed on appeal. Although state laws may not create classifications that are entirely without foundation, the referendum's distinction between terminally ill and other patients is not so arbitrary or irrational that it bears no relationship to a legitimate state goal. If a right to assisted suicide were recognized as a matter of constitutional law, no basis would exist for limiting the right to the terminally ill. However, if the legislature or public adopts that distinction as a matter of public policy, the judgment is entitled to deference under a rational relationship standard of review.

The appellate court is likely to apply the same deference to an assessment of the sufficiency of the safeguards under the law to prevent incapacitated, nonterminally ill individuals from committing suicide. Despite the weakness of the safeguards, especially the striking failure to protect patients from negligent physician conduct, the rational relationship test leaves little room for courts to second guess judgments that are principally matters of public policy. The courts will be especially reluctant to resolve a morally contested issue like assisted suicide on constitutional grounds—either by granting or by denying the right—when the legislature or broader public has reached its own judgment on the policy issues at stake.

Conclusion

To date, the three pending cases seeking to establish a right to assisted suicide have reached the same result, rejecting the contention that assisted suicide is constitutionally protected. As a matter of both precedent and policy, this conclusion is correct. The fact that the Constitution guarantees individuals the right to reject unwanted invasive procedures and to die a natural death does not mean that states must also authorize physicians to dispense lethal medications at a patient's request. Such a dramatic change in law would pose serious risks for vulnerable individuals, and could not plausibly be limited to the terminally ill.

Fortunately, most people vastly overestimate the number of terminally or chronically ill individuals who actually want to take their own lives. From the perspective of good health, many individuals believe that they would opt for suicide rather than endure a significantly diminished quality of life. Yet, once patients are confronted with illness, continued life often becomes more precious; given access to appropriate relief from pain and other debilitating symptoms, many of those who consider suicide during the course of a terminal illness abandon their desire for a quicker death in favor of a longer life made more tolerable with effective treatment. Rather than authorizing physicians to administer lethal medications to patients in despair, society should ensure that treatment for pain and depression is the norm, rather than the exception, for all individuals who are suffering.

References

1. Ga. Code Ann. § 16-5-5(b) (1993); 111. Ann. Stat. ch. 38, § 12-31(a)(1)–(2) (Smith-Hurd 1993); Ind. Code Ann. § 35-42-1-2.5 (West 1993); and Tenn. Code Ann. § 39-13-2 (1993).

2. See *Lee v. Oregon*, 891 F.Supp. 1429 (D. Or. 1995) (enjoining the law from going into effect); see also *infra* note 63 and accompanying text.

3. *Compassion in Dying v. State of Washington*, 850 F.Supp. 1454 (W.D. Wash. 1994).

4. *Compassion in Dying v. State of Washington*, 49 F.3d 586, *reh'g en banc granted*, 62 F.3d 299 (9th Cir. 1995).

5. *Quill v. Koppell*, 870 F.Supp. 78 (S.D.N.Y. 1994).

6. *People v. Kevorkian*, 527 N.W.2d 714 (Mich. 1994), *cert. denied*, 115 S.Ct. 1795 (1995).

7. *Cruzan v. Director, Missouri Dep't of Health*, 497 U.S. 261 (1990).

8. See, for example, *Austin v. Michigan State Chamber of Commerce*, 494 U.S. 652, 666 (1990).

9. *Youngberg v. Romeo*, 457 U.S. 307, 320 (1982).

10. See, for example, *Concrete Pipe & Products of California, Inc. v. Construction Laborers Pension Trust*, 113 S.Ct. 2264 (1993).

11. See *Cruzan*, 497 U.S. at 277. For an early articulation of this common law principle, see *Schloendorff v. Society of N.Y. Hosp.*, 105 N.E. 92 (1914) (Cardozo, J.) ("[E]very individual of sound mind and adult years has a right to determine what should be done with his own body.").

12. See, for example, *In re Colyer*, 660 P.2d 738 (1983) (affirming order authorizing removal of respirator from woman in persistent vegetative state); *In re Eichner*, 438 N.Y.S.2d 266 (authorizing the withdrawal of a respirator from an eighty-three-year-old permanently unconscious man who had clearly expressed his opposition to the artificial prolongation of his life), *cert. denied*, 454 U.S. 858 (1981); and *In re Spring*, 405 N.E.2d 115 (1980) (authorizing termination of hemodialysis treatment for seventy-seven-year-old man with advanced senility and end-stage kidney disease).

13. Note, "Physician-Assisted Suicide and the Right to Die with Assistance," *Harvard Law Review*, 105 (1992): at 2021.

14. *Id.* at 2029 ("[T]he physician's act—turning off the respirator—*is* a cause-in-fact of the death: but for turning off the machine, the patient would be alive today."); see also J. Fletcher, "The Courts and Euthanasia," *Law, Medicine & Health Care*, 15 (1987/88): at 225 ("[T]he primary causative act is the moral one of removing the supports.").

15. Note, *supra* note 13, at 2028–29.

16. *Compassion in Dying,* 850 F.Supp. at 1461.

17. See, for example, *Colyer,* 660 P.2d at 743 ("A death which occurs after the removal of life sustaining systems is from natural causes, neither set in motion nor intended by the patient."); and *Brophy v. New England Sinai Hosp., Inc.,* 497 N.E.2d 626 (1986) (following *Colyer*).

18. See, for example, *In re Conroy,* 486 A.2d 1209, 1224 (1985) (arguing that, although death might result from the refusal of treatment, "it would be the result, primarily, of the underlying disease, and not the result of a self-inflicted injury."); and *McKay v. Bergstedt,* 801 P.2d 617 (1990) (following *Conroy*).

19. See, for example, *Colyer,* 660 P.2d at 743.

20. *Cruzan,* 497 U.S. at 280.

21. *Quill,* 870 F.Supp. at 83.

22. *Compassion in Dying,* 49 F.3d at 594.

23. *Compassion in Dying,* 850 F.Supp. at 1459–60.

24. *Planned Parenthood v. Casey,* 112 S.Ct. 2791 (1992).

25. *Compassion in Dying,* 850 F.Supp. at 1460.

26. A.M. Capron, "Easing the Passing," *Hastings Center Report* 24, no. 4 (1994): at 25.

27. *Bowers v. Hardwick,* 478 U.S. 186 (1986).

28. *Michael H. v. Gerald D.,* 491 U.S. 110 (1989) (plurality opinion).

29. T.J. Marzen et al., "Suicide: A Constitutional Right?" *Duquesne Law Review* 24 (1985): at 76.

30. See L.O. Gostin, "Drawing a Line Between Killing and Letting Die: The Law, and Law Reform, on Medically Assisted Dying," *Journal of Law, Medicine & Ethics* 21 (1993): 94–101.

31. American Law Institute, *Model Penal Code and Commentaries* (Philadelphia: American Law Institute, Vol. 2, 1980): § 210.5, comment at 94 (concluding that "there is no form of criminal punishment that is acceptable for a completed suicide and that criminal punishment is singularly inefficacious to deter attempts to commit suicide"). See generally J.A. Alesandro, Comment, "Physician-Assisted Suicide and New York Law," *Albany Law Review* 57 (1994): 820–925.

32. *Kevorkian,* 527 N.W.2d at 733.

33. *Compassion in Dying,* 49 F.3d at 590.

34. See, for example, *Colyer,* 660 P.2d at 743.

35. *Bowers,* 478 U.S. at 186. See generally R. West, "The Ideal of Liberty," *University of Pennsylvania Law Review* 139 (1991): at 1373 (commenting on the "conservative" nature of traditional constitutional jurisprudence).

36. For a thorough discussion of the interests at stake, see New York State Task Force on Life and the Law, *When Death Is Sought: Assisted Suicide and Euthanasia in the Medical Context* (New York: New York State Task Force on Life and the Law, 1994): at 121–34.

37. R. Sedler, "The Constitution and Hastening Inevitable Death," *Hastings Center Report* 23, no. 5 (1993): 22–25.

38. Y. Conwell and E.D. Caine, "Rational Suicide and the Right to Die: Reality and Myth," *N. Engl. J. Med.*, 325 (1991): 1100–03. For an overview of clinical data on the relationship between suicide and untreated depression and pain, see New York State Task Force, *supra* note 36, at 9–47.

39. W. Breitbart, "Psychiatric Management of Cancer Pain," *Cancer* 63 (1989): 2336–42; and J.C. Holland, Chief, Psychiatry Services, Memorial Sloan-Kettering Cancer Center, Letter to the New York State Task Force on Life and the Law, Aug. 16, 1993.

40. A. Jacox et al., *Management of Cancer Pain, Clinical Practice Guideline No. 9* (Rockville: DHHS, AHCPR No. 94-0592, Mar. 1994): at 8; and M.Z. Solomon et al., "Decisions Near the End of Life: Professional Views on Life-Sustaining Treatments," *American Journal of Public Health* 83 (1993): at 18–19.

41. NIH Consensus Development Panel on Depression in Late Life, "Diagnosis and Treatment of Depression in Late Life," *JAMA* 268 (1992): 1018–24.

42. New York State Task Force, *supra* note 36, at 43–47.

43. C.S. Cleeland et al., "Pain and Its Treatment in Outpatients with Metastatic Cancer," *N. Engl. J. Med.* 330 (1994): 592–96.

44. See, for example, American Medical Association, Council on Ethical and Judicial Affairs, "Black-White Disparities in Health Care," *JAMA* 263 (1990): 2344–46; and R.J. Blendon et al., "Access to Medical Care for Black and White Americans," *JAMA* 261 (1989): 278–81.

45. M.A. Rodwin, "Conflicts in Managed Care," *N. Engl. J. Med.* 332 (1995): 604–07.

46. *Compassion in Dying,* 49 F.3d at 592.

47. R.K. Portenoy et al., "Determinants of the Willingness to Endorse Assisted Suicide: A Survey of Physicians, Nurses, and Social Workers," unpublished, 1994 (on file with the New York State Task Force on Life and the Law).

48. New York State Task Force, *supra* note 36, at 123.

49. L. Kass, "Why Doctors Must Not Kill," *Commonweal* 118, no. 14, supp. (1991): at 473.

50. *Compassion in Dying,* 49 F.3d at 592.

51. See, for example, T.E. Quill, C.K. Cassel, and D.E. Meier, "Care of the Hopelessly Ill: Proposed Clinical Criteria for Physician-Assisted Suicide," *N. Engl. J. Med.* 327 (1992): 1380–84.

52. See Y. Kamisar, "Are Laws Against Assisted Suicide Unconstitutional?" *Hastings Center Report* 23, no. 3 (1993): 32; and Y. Kamisar, "Assisted Suicide and Euthanasia: The Cases Are in the Pipeline," *Trial,* Dec. (1994): 30–35.

53. See, for example, *New York Transit Auth. v. Beazer,* 440 U.S. 568 (1979) (upholding an absolute ban on employment of users of narcotic drugs, including methadone users, despite the fact that the ban did not apply to patients in methadone treatment programs, because "any special rule short of total exclusion . . . is likely to be less precise.").

54. *United States v. Lee,* 455 U.S. 252, 259 (1982).

55. S. Kreimer, "Does Pro-Choice Mean Pro-Kevorkian? An Essay on *Roe, Casey,* and the Right to Die," *American University Law Review* 44 (1995): at 803.

56. *Conroy,* 486 A.2d at 1209.

57. *Fosmire v. Nicoleau,* 551 N.Y.S.2d 876 (1990).

58. *Compassion in Dying,* 49 F.3d at 591.

59. T.E. Quill, "The Care of Last Resort," *New York Times,* July 23, 1994, at A19.

60. See generally H. Hendin, "Seduced by Death: Doctors, Patients, and the Dutch Cure," *Issues in Law & Medicine* 10 (1994): 123–68.

61. L. Tribe, *American Constitutional Law* (New York: Foundation Press, 2d ed., 1988): § 15-11, at 1370.

62. *Cruzan,* 497 U.S. at 261 (Brennan, W., dissenting).

63. *Lee,* 891 F.Supp. at 1429.

64. *Id.* at 1437.

8

Physician-Assisted Suicide Should Be Legalized

Judy Harrow

Judy Harrow holds a master's degree in counseling. She is both a Wiccan high priestess and a cancer spouse.

Individuals who are suffering great pain and deterioration from illnesses, whether terminal or not, should have a legal option to use assisted suicide. Each person should be free to decide whether life is still worth living and to commit suicide if he or she chooses so. Furthermore, incapacitated persons who have decided to commit suicide should legally have access to assistance in carrying out the act.

> *Dying is personal. And it is profound. For many, the thought of an ignoble end, steeped in decay, is abhorrent. A quiet, proud death, bodily integrity intact, is a matter of extreme consequence.[1]*

We're all going to die. Those who work with the dying—doctors, nurses, counselors, and clergy—tell us that people seem to want just a few simple things at the end. They want to be as free from pain as possible. They want to be as autonomous as possible, in charge of the process if not of the outcome. Most important, they want the comforting presence and support of their loved ones. They do not want to be alone or among strangers at the end.

Our laws against assisted suicide have denied dying people these few bits of final comfort. Instead the dying have been offered a series of ugly choices: They can go the full, miserable route. They can choose a quick and clean end, but die alone. Or they can expose their loved ones to severe legal risk.

"One day at a time" only has meaning when a person has a choice. Listening to two cancer patients casually talking about where they hide their little bottles of "insurance," I realized the importance of autonomy. People who are confident that they can quit whenever it gets to be too much, and who still have things they want to do and friends to stand by

From Judy Harrow, "Neo-Pagan Ethics and Assisted Suicide," *Gnosis*, Winter 1997. Copyright ©1997 by Judy Harrow. An expanded version of this article will appear in the anthology *The Pagan Book of Living and Dying*, edited by Starhawk and Macha NightMare, forthcoming from HarperCollins.

them, can often keep going far beyond their own expectations. No law can force an ambulatory person to live longer than they want to. That's why most anti-suicide laws have long since been dropped from the books. The only laws that remain are those against helping others to commit suicide. Assuring people the right to *assisted* suicide simply means that the choice is still theirs even after they are physically incapacitated.

Sixty-two-year-old George Delury is in jail. His wife of 22 years, Myrna Lebov, was quadriplegic and entering dementia. By all medical estimates, her life expectancy was another ten to twenty years. She didn't want to experience another decade or two of mindlessness and hopelessness. So, at her request, he mixed a lethal potion, steadied it so she could drink it through a straw, then held her as she fell asleep for the last time. May we all find lovers as devoted!

Assisted suicide and the courts

The existing laws against assisted suicide do not save lives; they cruelly prolong deaths. They hold people in needless physical and emotional anguish. Thankfully, as social consensus is changing, so is the law.

Since the 1990 Supreme Court ruling in the case of *Cruzan v. Director,* it has been legal for a patient to refuse all artificial life support. People can now choose to die of starvation, thirst, or asphyxiation, with their doctor's help. Mind you, this is not legally considered suicide.

Notice, too, that after the withdrawal of life support systems, dying can take days or weeks. The patient may be drugged into complete unconsciousness, far past suffering. This does not, however, give any relief for the emotional pain of the family keeping watch.

Even so, *Cruzan* represented a great improvement over the days when months and years of life support were legally mandated even in entirely hopeless cases. The next step is currently in progress as the courts seem to be removing the artificial distinction between life-support withdrawal and assisted suicide.

> The writing of a prescription to hasten death, after consultation with a patient, involves a far less active role for the physician than is required in bringing about death through asphyxiation, starvation and/or dehydration. Withdrawal of life support requires physicians or those acting at their direction physically to remove equipment and, often, to administer palliative drugs which may themselves contribute to death. The ending of life by these means is nothing more nor less than assisted suicide.[2]

In the spring of 1996, two different circuits of the United States Court of Appeals overturned state laws prohibiting actively assisted suicide.[3] Both decisions are being appealed to the Supreme Court, which, at this writing in the summer of 1996, was expected to hear arguments in the fall. If the circuit court decisions are affirmed, doctor-assisted suicide will become legally available to patients who are both terminally ill and mentally competent.[4]

That's another big improvement, but it's still not good enough. Those qualifiers, "mentally competent" and "terminally ill," sound reasonable on first hearing. But imagine yourself as a hopelessly suffering patient who doesn't fit the profile.

A person is considered to be terminally ill when they are, by their doctor's best estimate, within six months of death. Myrna Lebov was not terminally ill. If we limit the privilege to people who would soon be dead anyhow, other people who, like Lebov, are facing long periods of restriction, deterioration, and pain are denied relief:

> The suicide of Nobel Prize winning physicist Percy Bridgman, recounted in one of the amicus briefs, graphically illustrates the point. Dr. Bridgman, 79, was in the final stages of cancer when he shot himself on August 20, 1961, leaving a suicide note that said: "It is not decent for society to make a man do this to himself. Probably this is the last day I will be able to do it myself."[5]

What about "mentally competent"? The bitter fact is that some diseases take away our minds. Many of us dread dementia far more than we do death. Are we not to be allowed an escape?

The legal argument for freedom of choice at the end of life can be made on the most simple practical and humanitarian terms, without reference to religion. Ethical and spiritual considerations reinforce the case further.

The great American tradition of freedom of religion should protect free choice. Many of us are religious, and we seem to become increasingly religious as we approach the great mystery of death. Different religions have different teachings about how dying people should conduct themselves. Some are quite specific, but none can legitimately bind nonadherents. So tolerance for a wide range of choice at the end of life is a necessary part of living together in a religiously pluralistic community. As an American, I am for tolerance.

No law can force an ambulatory person to live longer than they want to.

As a Neo-Pagan, even beyond supporting full tolerance for the religiously dictated choices of others, I insist upon complete freedom of choice for myself. My religion does not prescribe any one right way to die. Pagan ethics are situational on principle. Our core statement, our Golden Rule, is the Wiccan Rede: "An it harm none, do what you will." While committed to a personal ethic of harmlessness, we resist any arbitrary restriction on personal autonomy. People should be free to do anything they want, including end their lives, unless it's clear that doing so will harm others. So, from religious conviction, I oppose many kinds of antichoice legislation.

A word of caution here: While opposing well-meant but ill-considered laws that take away our choices, we need to bear in mind that the law does have a proper role: to protect our right to choose against undue outside influence.

The *Cruzan* decision, which permitted the withdrawal of life-support systems, also allowed states to set strict standards for assuring that the will of the patient was being followed, not that of the family, the institution, or—perish the thought!—the insurance company.

There is a real danger, with the advent of profit-driven "managed care," that case managers will press the more vulnerable (poor and/or solitary) patients to commit suicide early in order to improve the "bottom line." Those of us who claim freedom of choice at the end of life, as at its beginning, need to be very careful that choice is truly free rather than dictated by economics.

Many of us dread dementia far more than we do death.

The government exists to defend and develop those interests which we, as a community, hold in common: things like public safety, environmental protection, and the maintenance of as much of a "social safety net" as we decide we want. Although we have no collective interest in prolonging anybody's dying, we have a very real interest in assuring that every patient's wishes are honored. Only thus can we make sure that our own wishes will be honored when our time comes.

When there are no more laws about suicide, there will be even more need for conscientious personal decision. If society isn't choosing for us, we have to choose for ourselves. The word "right" is ambiguous. It means both something that is "due to a person by law, tradition, or nature" and something that is "fitting, proper, or appropriate."[6] Although we have the *right* to do something, it may not always be the *right* thing to do.

Because this choice has not been in our own hands, there is not much tradition to guide us. Hence today it's easier and saner to think about such hard issues before we have to actually decide. Without forcing our choices on each other, we can share our thoughts and feelings. Already discussion is beginning in both the medical and counseling professions about the situational ethics of assisted suicide.[7]

We need to be talking about this issue within our respective faith communities as well. Different religions will have very different teachings, based on their different understandings of this life and the next. Those who believe in some form of purgatory, for example, may feel that there is merit in suffering, or that the Deity's will is not to be evaded.

Guidelines for considering assisted suicide

What can Neo-Pagans learn from the Rede? Harmlessness comes first. Doing whatever we can to minimize any needless trauma to our loved ones precedes the exercise of personal will. Here are a few suggestions:

• A person considering suicide should take some time over the decision. After all, once done, it cannot be undone. Suicide is not a decision to be made in panic upon first hearing a frightening diagnosis. A cooling-off period can also be used to make some responsible preparations.

• Patients should have full medical information. What is their prognosis? What are their treatment options? Is there any realistic hope for a cure? How long can they expect a reasonable quality of life? Can their symptoms be mitigated? Can their pain be controlled by methods that still allow for creative self-expression and loving interaction with their dear ones?

• Have they taken care of all possible practical business? Have they paid all possible debts, made or updated their will, made all possible funeral arrangements? Rational and honorable suicide means leaving as little work or worry as possible to one's survivors.

• Have they come to closure with as many of their emotional issues as possible? Have they made peace in as many of their relationships as they can? Are they clear in conscience that they have made their best efforts toward peace and healing?

• Have they discussed their decision to commit suicide with all their close significant others, allowing those people time to adjust to the choice?

Notice that most of this is a matter of taking care of business, both psychological and practical: good practice at any stage of life, whether or not we are ill. These things clear the way for an honorable decision, but they do not decide the issue one way or the other.

We resist any arbitrary restriction on personal autonomy.

There may still be some purpose in remaining, even in a damaged and hurting body. Although Pagans do not value suffering for its own sake, many of us are committed to being "willing to suffer to learn." So the ultimate question, for me, is when does learning end?

There is always beauty around us, always something to learn. The Ancient Ones are always among and within us. The Source is infinite, but our receptors are finite. We interact with this glorious world through our bodies, and bodies wear out. Eventually our abilities to perceive, enjoy, and learn are irretrievably gone. The decision to leave can only be made from *within* a failing body. No one else can ever know; no one else should ever choose.

Notes

1. *Cruzan v. Director*, 497 US 261 (1990); Justice Brennan's dissent.

2. *Quill v. Vacco*, U.S. Court of Appeals, Second Circuit, April 1996.

3. *Compassion in Dying v. State of Washington*, U.S. Court of Appeals, Ninth Circuit, March 1996, and *Quill v. Vacco*.

4. In June of 1997, the Supreme Court overruled the decisions of both circuit courts. They held that the Constitution neither grants nor forbids the right to physician-assisted suicide. So the issue is returned to the democratic process and the "laboratory" of the states.

5. Sherwin B. Nuland, *How We Die: Reflections on Life's Final Chapter* (New York: Knopf, 1993), pp. 152–53; quoted in the *Compassion in Dying* decision.

6. *American Heritage Dictionary*, third ed.

7. Timothy E. Quill, M.D., Christine K. Cassel, M.D., and Diane E. Meier, M.D., "Care for the Hopelessly Ill: Clinical Criteria for Physician-Assisted Suicide," in *The New England Journal of Medicine* (Nov. 5, 1992); and James L. Werth, "Rational Suicide Reconsidered: AIDS as an Impetus for Change," in *Death Studies*, 19:65–80 (1995).

9

Physician-Assisted Suicide Should Not Be Legalized

Leon R. Kass

Leon R. Kass is Addie Clark Harding Professor in the College and the Committee on Social Thought at the University of Chicago.

The legalization of physician-assisted suicide would be unethical and dangerous. The doctor's role is that of a healer, not a killer. Physicians who assist patients in killing themselves would be compromising their duty to care for and benefit the sick. Furthermore, once physician-assisted suicide is legal for the terminally ill, it will be difficult to prevent the spread of the practice to those who are not terminally ill, such as the retarded or disabled. Managed care companies, which would profit from the hastened deaths of the chronically ill, would lobby aggressively for extending "the right to die a dignified death" to the mentally incompetent. The energy that is currently focused on attempts to legalize assisted suicide must be channeled into efforts to improve the care and comfort for the chronically and terminally ill.

R ecent efforts to legalize physician-assisted suicide and to establish a constitutional "right to die" are deeply troubling events, morally dubious in themselves, extremely dangerous in their likely consequences. The legalization of physician-assisted suicide, ostensibly a measure enhancing the freedom of dying patients, is in fact a deadly license for physicians to prescribe death, free from outside scrutiny and immune from possible prosecution. The manufacture of a "right to die," ostensibly a gift to those not dying fast enough, is, in fact, the state's abdication of its duty to protect innocent life and its abandonment especially of the old, the weak, and the poor.

The legalization of physician-assisted suicide will pervert the medical profession by transforming the healer of human beings into a technical dispenser of death. For over two millennia the medical ethic, mindful that power to cure is also power to kill, has held as an inviolable rule, "Doctors must not kill." The venerable Hippocratic Oath clearly rules out

From Leon R. Kass, "Dehumanization Triumphant," *First Things*, August/September 1996. Reprinted with permission.

physician-assisted suicide. Without this taboo, medicine ceases to be a trustworthy and ethical profession; without it, all of us will suffer—yes, more than we suffer now because some of us die too slowly.

The doctor-patient relationship will be damaged. The patient's trust in the doctor's devotion to the patient's best interests will be hard to sustain once doctors can legally prescribe death. Even conscientious physicians will have trouble caring wholeheartedly for patients once death becomes a "therapeutic option." The prohibition against killing patients, medicine's first principle of ethical self-restraint, recognizes that no physician devoted to the benefit of the sick can serve the patient by making him dead. The physician-suicide-assistant or physician-euthanizer is a deadly self-contradiction.

Physician-assisted suicide, once legal, will not stay confined to the terminally ill and mentally competent who freely and knowingly elect it for themselves. Requests will be engineered and choices manipulated by those who control the information, and, manipulation aside, many elderly and incurable people will experience a right to choose death *as their duty* to do so. Moreover, the vast majority of those who are said to "merit" "a humane and dignified death" do not fall in this category and cannot request it for themselves. Persons with mental illness or Alzheimer's disease, deformed infants, and retarded or dying children would thus be denied our new humane "aid-in-dying." But not to worry. The lawyers, encouraged by the cost-containers, will sue to rectify this inequity. Why, they will argue, should the comatose or the demented be denied a right to assisted suicide just because they cannot claim it for themselves? With court-appointed proxy consentors, we will quickly erase the distinction between the right to choose one's own death and the right to request someone else's.

The legalization of physician-assisted suicide will pervert the medical profession.

The termination of lives someone else thinks are no longer worth living is now occurring on a large scale in Holland, where assisted suicide and euthanasia have been practiced by physicians for more than a decade, under "safeguards" more stringent than those enacted in the Oregon law. [In 1994, Oregon voters approved a law that legalized physician-assisted suicide. The law was challenged in court. However, in October 1997 the Supreme Court upheld the law. Oregon voters reaffirmed the law in November 1997.] According to the Dutch government's own alarming figures, there are over one thousand cases per year of direct *non*voluntary euthanasia; also 8,100 cases of morphine overdosage intending to terminate life, 61 percent without the patient's consent. Although the guidelines insist that choosing death must be informed and voluntary, over 40 percent of Dutch physicians have performed involuntary euthanasia. As the Dutch have shown, the practice of assisted suicide is in principle unregulable, because it is cloaked in the privacy of the doctor-patient relationship.

Legalizing assisted suicide would mark a drastic change in the social and political order. The state would be surrendering its monopoly on the legal use of lethal force, a monopoly it holds under the social contract, a monopoly it needs if it is to protect innocent life, its first responsibility. It should surprise no one if physicians, once they are exempted from the ban on the private use of lethal force, wind up killing without restraint. Here, by the way, is a *genuine* violation of the Fourteenth Amendment: deprivation of *life* without due process of law.

We must care for the dying, not make them dead. By accepting mortality yet knowing that we will not kill, doctors can focus on enhancing the lives of those who are dying, with relief of pain and discomfort, moral and social support, and, when appropriate, the removal of technical interventions that are merely useless or degrading additions to the burdens of dying—including, frequently, hospitalization itself. Doctors must not intentionally kill, or help to kill, but they may allow a patient to die.

We must care for the dying, not make them dead.

Ceasing medical intervention, allowing nature to take its course, differs fundamentally from assisting suicide and active euthanasia. Not the physician, but the underlying fatal illness becomes the true cause of death. More important morally, in ceasing treatment the physician *does not intend the death* of the patient, even if death follows as a result. Rather, he seeks to avoid useless and degrading medical additions to the already sad end of a life. In contrast, in assisted suicide the physician necessarily intends primarily that the patient be made dead.

One cannot exaggerate the importance of the distinction between withholding or withdrawing treatment and directly killing, a distinction foolishly dismissed in the recent Court of Appeals' decisions. Both as a matter of law and as a matter of medical ethics, the right to refuse unwanted medical intervention is properly seen not as part of a right to become dead but rather as part of a *right protecting how we choose to live,* even while we are dying.

Once we refuse the technical fix, physicians and the rest of us can also rise to the occasion: we can learn to act humanly in the presence of finitude. Far more than adequate morphine and the removal of burdensome chemotherapy, the dying need our presence and our encouragement. Withdrawal of human contact, affection, and care is the greatest single cause of the dehumanization of dying. People who care for autonomy and dignity should try to correct this dehumanization of the end of life, instead of giving dehumanization its final triumph by welcoming the desperate good-bye-to-all-that contained in one final plea for poison. Not the alleged humaneness of an elixir of death, but the humanness of connected living-while-dying is what medicine—and the rest of us—most owe the dying. The treatment of choice is and always will be company and care.

10

Legal Safeguards Can Prevent Physician-Assisted Suicide from Harming Society

David Orentlicher

David Orentlicher, a lawyer and physician, is an associate professor at Indiana University School of Law, Indianapolis, and acting director of the Center for Health Care Ethics and Professionalism at the School of Medicine. He was formerly director of the American Medical Association's Division of Medical Ethics.

Critics of doctor-assisted suicide often support their positions by pointing out the potential for abuse of the practice. They are concerned that doctors or insurance companies may pressure patients to choose suicide or that doctors may not be qualified to distinguish rational from irrational aid-in-dying requests. While these concerns are valid, abuse can be prevented with appropriate regulations and safeguards. For example, states could require thorough and systematic evaluations by psychiatric specialists of each patient requesting aid-in-dying to determine if their decision to die was freely chosen and rational. Because physician-assisted suicide can be effectively regulated, it should be legalized so terminally ill patients can have a legitimate option to end their suffering.

After years of debate, prompted by high-profile cases such as those involving Jack Kevorkian, our laws may soon widely recognize a right to physician-assisted suicide. Two federal appeals courts, with jurisdictions including New York, California, and nine other states, have recently held that terminally ill patients have a constitutional right to this way of ending life. And in Oregon, a public referendum has resulted in the enactment of a statutory right to assisted suicide for terminally ill residents.

Opponents of assisted suicide—including the American Medical As-

From David Orentlicher, "Navigating the Narrows of Doctor-Assisted Suicide," *Technology Review*, July 1996. Reprinted with permission from MIT's *Technology Review* magazine, copyright 1996.

sociation—have argued that its legalization poses serious threats to the welfare of patients and the ethics of the medical profession. While most of the concerns do not hold up under scrutiny, some are valid and must be addressed through stringent safeguards.

Many commentators say there is no need for assisted suicide as long as doctors provide adequate pain control. These observers point out that more needs to be done to ensure that dying patients receive enough medication for their pain. Still, some patients' pain cannot be alleviated even with the most aggressive treatment. More important, physical pain is not the only cause of intolerable suffering. Many dying patients want to end their lives because of their utter dependence on others, the wasting of the body into little more than flesh and bones, the loss of control over bodily functions, the unrelieved mental and physical exhaustion, and the knowledge that things will only grow worse.

People who oppose doctor-assisted suicide have also pointed out the real risk that the practice may extend to inappropriate cases. Vulnerable patients could ask to end their lives because of pressures from family, caregivers, or insurers, and they may be influenced by arguments about the burden that treatment for dying patients places on society's limited resources. Patients seeking assisted suicide may be suffering from treatable depression or the side effects of medication, and doctors might not always be adequately trained to distinguish requests that are rational from those that are not. Moreover, physicians sometimes find that caring for patients who are seriously ill is time-consuming and psychologically draining, and may thus respond to entreaties for assisted suicide too readily.

Society should address these possibilities with safeguards rather than a prohibition, just as has been done when requests for withdrawal of life-sustaining treatment have posed similar risks. A specialist in pain relief and other palliative measures should ensure that all appropriate care has been provided to patients asking for the means to hasten the dying process. To ensure that a request for assisted suicide is truly voluntary and not the result of moral incapacity or undue pressure, a psychiatric specialist should fully evaluate the requesting patient. And a social-services specialist should determine that all other support services have been considered, such as home hospice care, which some patients might prefer over assisted suicide.

> *Society should address [the risks posed by physician-assisted suicide] with safeguards rather than a prohibition.*

Still, critics point out that some doctors might want to disregard such safeguards. Multiple consultations take time and cost money, and physicians may be tempted to shortcut the process. The risks of abuse are real, according to findings from the Netherlands, where doctor-assisted suicide and euthanasia are practiced. In 1991 researchers reported that Dutch physicians had not fulfilled the country's procedural requirements in more than 25 percent of the cases involving these methods of dying. But the United States can avoid a similar experience. Since in Holland the primary abuse has been the administration of euthanasia by doctors without the patient's clear consent, U.S. laws can continue to prohibit euthanasia and insist that the right to assisted suicide be limited to patients who can self-administer the fatal dose of medication. While this requirement would deny death to patients so incapacitated they cannot take drugs by themselves, the right to assisted suicide should not be extended too far.

Laws should permit doctors to assist in the suicide only of terminally ill patients.

Moreover, laws should permit doctors to assist in the suicide only of terminally ill patients. Such a limitation would not only restrict the procedure to a justified group but would also tie the practice to the reason society has strongly supported a right to refuse life-sustaining treatment. For example, in its 1976 landmark opinion in the case of Karen Quinlan, the New Jersey Supreme Court observed that treatment withdrawal should be permitted when the patient's prognosis becomes very poor and the degree of bodily invasion from treatment becomes very high. To ensure that a person has reached such a stage, a second, independent physician with expertise in the patient's illness should confirm any diagnosis and prognosis.

To a certain extent, the courts can implement safeguards for assisted suicide. But years may be needed for cases to work themselves through all levels of appeals, and court decisions often address only part of an issue at a time. Legislatures can move more quickly, and should address the topic of assisted suicide comprehensively after analyzing the full range of perspectives. State legislatures should handle this issue because experimentation by different states will help sort out the best approaches, a process the courts have long held important.

As legislatures and the courts develop and insist on safeguards, they would do well to recognize that permitting doctor-assisted suicide will actually prolong some patients' lives. What patients often want is not so much the ability to die but the knowledge that they have control over the timing of their death. Once such control is permitted, they may be more willing to undergo aggressive medical treatments that are painful and risky. If a treatment does not succeed but only worsens the patient's condition, the person is assured that he or she can end the suffering.

We have already seen the life-prolonging effects of patient control. Both Elizabeth Bouvia, who depended on a feeding tube, and Lawrence McAfee, who required a ventilator, sued to have their treatment stopped. But neither exercised that right once the courts recognized it. The two were willing to continue their lives upon receiving clear authority that they could decide whether and when their treatment would end.

By adopting stringent safeguards for doctor-assisted suicide, society can give dying patients the fundamental ability to decide how they wish to handle their suffering. And it can provide the critical assurance that they are protected from abuse.

11

Legalizing Physician-Assisted Suicide Would Harm Society

Wesley J. Smith

Wesley J. Smith, a California attorney, is the author of Forced Exit: The Slippery Slope from Assisted Suicide to Legalized Murder.

The legalization of physician-assisted suicide would create an unethical, dangerous, and controlling policy that would adversely affect society. There is little evidence to suggest that proposed assisted suicide guidelines would prevent abuses by the medical profession and family members. Recent court decisions indicate that if assisted suicide were legalized, the practice would not be limited to the mentally competent and terminally ill; people who are incompetent to make their own decisions, including children, might eventually have appointed guardians making the decision to end their lives. In addition, the healthcare industry, having millions of its dollars at stake, would have a tremendous and unrestricted incentive to encourage premature deaths in order to avoid the costs of lengthy treatments. The legalization of assisted suicide will come at an enormous cost to society. It must be prevented.

Without question, the campaign to legalize "physician-assisted suicide" has been on a roll. In 1996, two U.S. courts of appeals ruled that laws prohibiting assisted suicide are unconstitutional.[1] As I write, both cases are on appeal to the Supreme Court, but several current opinion polls indicate that support for legalizing assisted suicide ranges as high as 70 percent. [In June 1997, the Supreme Court ruled against the two U.S. courts of appeals decisions and declared that physician-assisted suicide is not a constitutional right.]

Meanwhile, in Michigan, Jack "Doctor Death" Kevorkian has been acquitted of the crime of assisted suicide in three separate trials, despite his own insistence that he is guilty as charged.

Does all this mean that legalization is inevitable, just a matter of

From Wesley J. Smith, "Inevitable Assisted Suicide? Don't Bet Your Life," *Human Life Review*, Spring 1997. Reprinted with permission.

time? Not on your life. History shows that the more people dig beneath the surface and learn the *truth* about assisted suicide and euthanasia, the less they like it. Indeed, the few popular referendums on the issue that have been held in this country have all followed this pattern.

In 1991, Initiative 119, which would have legalized active euthanasia, was voted on in the state of Washington. Early polls showed popular support for the measure in excess of 70 percent. Yet, once opponents were able to focus the debate and present the in-depth reasons to oppose legalization, the initiative lost by 54-46, a precipitous drop of approximately 25 percent in popularity in just a few months.

Similarly, in 1992, California's Proposition 161—a measure virtually identical to Initiative 119—began with more than 70 percent support. Once again, when the disturbing facts about euthanasia were presented in detail, voters saw the light and the proposal lost by the identical 54-46 margin. Even the 1994 passage of Measure 16 in Oregon, which legalized physician-assisted suicide (PAS) in that state, only passed with a bare 51 percent of the vote after initial polling again showed support of nearly 70 percent—the decline occurring despite what was generally considered an ineffective opposition campaign that many observers believe would have been successful had it been more aggressively run. Moreover, although it has been little noted in the media, four states—Virginia, Rhode Island, Iowa, and Louisiana—have passed laws outlawing assisted suicide after the passage of Measure 16. (For more, see my "Unnecessary Tragedy: Assisted Suicide Comes to Oregon," in the Spring 1995 issue of *Human Life Review.*)

This general pattern should not make us sanguine, however. Measure 16 tragically proved the truth of the old *cliché* that close only counts in horseshoes. If the law goes into effect, which as of this writing appears likely (a federal judge had ruled that Measure 16 was unconstitutional,[2] but a court of appeals recently overturned the verdict, stating that those opposed to the measure did not have the standing to sue[3]), it will not matter whether Measure 16 passed by one vote or one million votes; the state will cease to protect the lives of the weakest and most vulnerable Oregonians, permitting doctors to participate in the intentional ending of human lives. [Measure 16 was upheld by the Supreme Court in October 1997. In a November 1997 referendum, Oregon voters reaffirmed their support for the law.]

Why does legalizing PAS apparently have broad, albeit shallow and changeable, popular appeal? Many streams have come together at this particular time to form the cultural river that nourishes what I call the "death culture." First and foremost, perhaps, is the elevation of personal autonomy as society's overriding value. It used to be that individualism, certainly a venerable American trait, was kept in perspective as one important value among several—such as our obligation to watch out for each other (communitarianism) and support in particular circumstances for policies that curtail individual behavior to benefit the common good (for example, laws prohibiting heroin use)—that traditionally formed the dynamic system of responsible American freedom that our founding fathers called "ordered liberty."

Today however, for many Americans, personal autonomy has become *the* overriding value, rather than one value among many. Knowing this, pro-euthanasia activists pepper their advocacy with the lexicon of individualism. This is planting seed in fertile ground: for many people, say the magic word "choice" and nothing more need be said; the argument is over.

Another driving force behind the euthanasia movement is the issue of "control." At the same time that "hastened death" is hoisted high as a banner of liberty, proponents exploit people's fear of death and the suffering that can accompany serious illness, promising that by choosing the time and manner of death the grim reaper will be somehow tamed. In this atmosphere, dying naturally, if it involves discomfort or time, is increasingly promoted as a "bad" death. On the other hand, hastened death is presented as empowering, courageous, and noble.

The more people dig beneath the surface and learn the truth about assisted suicide and euthanasia, the less they like it.

The increase in the popularity of euthanasia is also a vote of no confidence in the medical profession. Many supporters are afraid, nay terrified, at the prospect of being victimized at the hands of an out-of-control doctor, who they fear will "hook them up to machines" and force them to suffer as cash cows lingering in an agonizing limbo until they die—or their health insurance runs out—whichever comes first. This is not irrational. Too many people have seen their loved ones allowed to writhe in pain that could have been relieved, too many have had their own suffering ignored, and too many have been treated impersonally and dismissively in their time of greatest need by "health care professionals."

Then there is the issue of compassion, a virtue on which some euthanasia advocates claim a monopoly. By exaggerating the travails of disability and dying, proponents of legalized killing claim that all they seek to do is eliminate suffering, ignoring or downplaying the many dignified, compassionate and effective means that exist today to reduce or eliminate pain and suffering *without* eliminating the patient.

A less visible but especially dangerous force driving the euthanasia juggernaut is simply money. Our health-care system is quickly transforming from what is called "fee for service" in which medical professionals earn money by treating people, to a system dominated by for-profit health maintenance organizations (HMOs), in which money is made by health-insurance companies primarily by reducing costs. In an HMO, a penny saved is literally a penny earned. That is why legalized euthanasia would be especially profitable to the fast-growing for-profit HMO industry. Thus, it may not be coincidental that many nonprofit health-care foundations with ties to for-profit health-care corporations finance behind-the-scenes propagandizing of the medical professions in favor of legalizing PAS.

Shallow reporting

Underlying it all is a sense of despair and nihilism arising from the disintegrating communities and loss of common values we find all around us.

Canadian newspaper columnist Andrew Coyne, reacting to the widespread public support of Robert Latimer (who killed his 12-year-old daughter because she was disabled by cerebral palsy), said it most eloquently and succinctly when he wrote: "A society that believes in nothing can offer no argument even against death. A culture that has lost its faith in life cannot comprehend why it should be endured."[4]

All of these themes can be accurately and effectively rebutted, given the time, space, and audience attention that such an effort requires, a process perhaps best summarized by the word "depth." Unfortunately, with people increasingly attracted to sensationalism, scandal, gossip, and the news as entertainment, depth has a low priority in our national discourse. Today, most people receive their information through the prism of media and popular culture grown increasingly tabloid in nature and sensationalistic in tone, long on emotionalism and woefully short on detail, often lacking both the substance and context required for informed decision-making.

This has certainly been true of the euthanasia issue. News reports, entertainment programs, and articles which deal with euthanasia almost always present it in a sympathetic light as the "only" choice available to alleviate a desperate patient's suffering. Popular television programs such as *ER, Homicide, Chicago Hope, Star Trek: Deep Space Nine, Star Trek Voyager* (in which we learn that Vulcans like Mr. Spock practice ritual suicide in old age) and *Law and Order,* just to name a few, have all aired programs with a euthanasia-sympathetic point of view.

[In Compassion in Dying *v.* Washington, *the Ninth Circuit Court of Appeals] opened the door for the killing of patients who are* incompetent.

Articles in popular magazines simultaneously present the same message, typified by an article in *The New Yorker* in which the writer extols his mother's assisted suicide, concluding, "Having seen the simple logic of euthanasia in action and witnessed the comfort of that control, what astonishes me is how many people die by other means."[5] Meanwhile, the popular "family values" magazine *Ladies' Home Journal* recently carried what it called a "roundtable" discussion of assisted suicide—but *nobody* around the table was *against* legalization![6]

The news media is generally no better at plumbing the depths of the issue. Increasingly driven by ratings and circulation concerns, to an increasing degree a "good story" is seen as one that is short on depth and long on emotionalism. If a sick person is assisted in suicide by a doctor or family member, that's *news!* Coverage focuses intently on the reasons the person wanted to die. Friends speak of his or her great suffering and courage in choosing suicide. At the same time, there is little (if *any*) investigation to discover whether the victim was receiving adequate medical care, proper pain control, or treatment for depression.

Most of the stories written about Jack Kevorkian's "assisted" killings are cases in point. Take the reporting of the September 3, 1996, death of Jack Leatherman, 73, who had pancreatic cancer. Newspaper reports, such as the one in the Boston *Globe,* not only reported the death and the nature of Leatherman's illness, but also printed the allegation by one of Kevorkian's henchmen that "No amount of pain relief could control the pain that he was suffering,"[7] a bogus claim that was *not* questioned or investigated. Had it been, reporters would have discovered that it was flat-out *wrong:* morphine pills are very effective in controlling the pain associated with pancreatic cancer, and in the rare event that opioids are insufficient to the task, a medical procedure can be performed to numb the nerve that transmits pain stimuli from the abdomen to the brain, thus eliminating all pain caused by the cancer.[8]

Stories that highlight the reasons to oppose legalization, with a few exceptions, generally do not receive equivalent coverage. Nor, again with a few exceptions, are these stories presented with the same levels of emotional intensity of drama. Indeed, if hospice care helps someone die a dignified, natural death in comfort and surrounded by a loving family, unless the person is famous it won't make the news at all. If a cancer patient is no longer suicidal because he received effective pain control, that too is not news—it's the proverbial dog-bites-man story, it's "normal." More, if a patient is somehow coerced into an "early death," it rarely becomes a public matter, since the abuser will not be anxious for public exposure.

All this is like the "death of a thousand cuts" to the traditional sanctity-of-life ethic. With the media and the various organs of popular culture generally playing the same tune—and with opposition voices generally limited to reactions to a Kevorkian killing or otherwise muted to a discordant note in the deep background—the awesome power of repetition, like ocean waves breaking against a rock, contributes individually and collectively to the gradual erosion of the belief in the sanctity of human life and toward an accepting and sympathetic attitude among the general public toward euthanasia. In such a *milieu*, it is little wonder that many public opinion polls indicate support for legalization.

The battle over euthanasia and assisted suicide is too important to be left to such shallow public discourse. Legalized killing has gone from a theoretical possibility to a genuine and realistic probability, with Oregon's law permitting assisted suicide likely to go into effect. [In 1994, Oregon voters approved a law that legalized physician-assisted suicide. The law was challenged in court. However, the Supreme Court upheld the law in October 1997, and Oregon voters reaffirmed their support for the measure in a November referendum.] That being so, as the New York *Times* columnist Peter Steinfels put it, the time has come for a deeper debate that "would focus on a different set of questions," bringing with it a "more realistic" tone.[9]

What are some of the issues that would be presented in such a deeper national discourse? Here is a sampling:

One of the more glaring misconceptions about the campaign to legalize euthanasia is that it would be "limited" to the "terminally ill" after all other options for relieving suffering have been attempted. Despite the fact that only some—one in five—victims would have died naturally within a few months, Jack Kevorkian is often described in the media as a doctor who helps terminally-ill people to commit assisted suicide.

Similarly, the media described the Ninth Circuit Court of Appeals *Compassion in Dying* v. *Washington* decision, mentioned earlier, which declared assisted suicide a fundamental liberty interest, as applying "only" to people who are "mentally competent" and "terminally ill." Yet to read the Court's opinion is to see that it explicitly opened the door to assisted suicide *for people with disabilities,* stating ". . . seriously impaired individuals will, along with non-impaired individuals, be the beneficiaries of the liberty interest asserted here." According to the decision, killing could also be based on *financial* considerations—the Court was "reluctant to say that, in a society in which the costs of protracted health care can be so exorbitant, it is improper for competent, terminally ill adults to take the economic welfare of their families and loved ones into consideration." The Court even opened the door for the killing of patients who are *incompetent* to make their own medical decisions (perhaps including *children*), stating in a footnote that "We should make it clear that a decision of a duly appointed surrogate decision maker, is for all legal purposes the decision of the patient himself."[10]

With so much money at stake, people need to think about euthanasia in the HMO context.

Political advocacy in favor of legalization is pushing this same agenda. Look closely at the more recent pro-euthanasia articles and the terms "hopelessly ill," "desperately ill," or "incurably ill" are frequently being used in place of "terminally ill." For example, Dr. Timothy Quill, one of the nation's preeminent euthanasia advocates, has advocated that assisted suicide be permitted for patients with "incurable" and "debilitating" conditions associated with "severe, unrelenting suffering"—in other words, allegedly-hopeless illness. It is also important to note that as used by Quill, the term "suffering" is not synonymous with "pain." Suffering can include such difficulties as the fear of future suffering, loss of dignity, and other such completely subjective criteria.[11]

Likewise, when the New York *Times* editorialized in favor of legalizing assisted suicide in the wake of the facilitated killing of Myrna Lebov (a Manhattan woman who had multiple sclerosis) by her husband, George Delury, the *Times* stated that the Delury matter "strengthens the case for allowing qualified medical professionals to assist *desperately ill patients* with no hope of recovery to die with dignity."[12] [My emphasis.] It is important to note that Myrna Lebov was indisputably *not* terminally ill.

So, who are the "hopelessly ill"? One common definition was published in the Summer 1995 issue of the journal *Suicide and Life Threatening Behavior,* based on a survey of psychiatrists who support the concept of rational suicide. By this definition, hopeless conditions "include but are not necessarily limited to, terminal illnesses, [maladies causing] severe physical and/or psychological pain, physically or mentally debilitating and/or deteriorating conditions [and circumstances where the quality of life is] no longer acceptable to the individual."[13] In other words, nearly every person experiencing a serious malady, from arthritis, diabetes, and chronic migraine to chronic depression, schizophrenia, HIV, and Alzheimer's disease—you name it—would be entitled to euthanasia under the "hopeless illness" category.

If the American people knew the breadth and scope of the euthanasia movement's true agenda, support for legalizing killing would likely drop like a stone thrown from a bridge.

Legalized assisted suicide would be especially dangerous in the money-driven U.S. health-care system

Ask people what they fear about end-of-life medical care, and most will say that they fear being kept alive involuntarily on machines long after the time had come to give up the ghost. Little noted in the debate over euthanasia is that the danger of such abuse is quickly *fading*. Why? Because, as I have already emphasized, our health-care system is being transformed from the traditional "fee for service"—in which medical professionals earn money by treating people—to a system dominated by for-profit health maintenance organizations (HMOs), in which money is made primarily by *reducing* costs.

If killing seriously ill or disabled patients becomes a legitimate method of "treatment," anyone who requires depth of care will be significantly endangered. Remember, for HMOs profits come from limiting costs, which means reducing services if possible. Imagine the money that could be saved by not treating cancer patients because they choose instead to be killed, or AIDS patients, or quadriplegics—this disturbing paradigm is one reason why managed care is now called "managed death" by those worried about legalized euthanasia in a health-care system dominated by HMOs.[14]

Studies prove that the [protective guidelines for euthanasia in the Netherlands] are completely ineffective.

To gauge the accuracy of this concern, we need only focus on the viselike cost-cutting pressure already being placed on doctors at the clinical level. One of the hallmarks of HMO care is the dual role of the plan member's "primary-care physician" (PCP). The PCP (or for children, a pediatrician) is the plan member's personal doctor, in charge of preventive care, managing chronic conditions, providing inoculations, and the like. But the PCP also serves a function on behalf of the HMO as the "gatekeeper" in charge of controlling the cost of each patient's care.

It is the gatekeeper function that has so many physicians and consumer advocates worried about financial conflicts-of-interest between doctors and their patients. Here's why: doctors in many HMOs are paid individually (or as part of a small group) on a "capitation" basis—the PCP (or the group) receives a flat monthly fee for each patient, regardless of the frequency of care the patient requires. Some capitation payments are extremely low, as little as $8 per month.[15] So if a patient required four visits per month, the doctor would be paid only $2 per consultation, a figure so low that it could discourage depth-of-care. Some companies go even farther, imposing a compensation system in which the PCP is *personally* held financially responsible by the HMO for any referrals made outside his group, to specialists, or for tests. In such contracts, the PCP receives a higher-than-usual capitation payment, perhaps $40 per month or so, but in return must *personally* pay for each patient's lab tests, consultations with specialists, and emergency care, up to a maximum per patient which may be as high as $5,000 (after which the HMO pays).[16] In a system where doctors lose money every time they refer a patient "out-of-house," they may be reluctant to allow their patients to consult specialists, including pain-control experts or psychiatrists—e.g., those crucial to the proper care of many dying or chronically-ill patients who, *without* such treatment, might indeed turn in despair to a "hastened" end.

Not coincidentally, Wall Street investors and for-profit HMO executives are getting rich from money made from draconian compensation controls that can be dangerous to their members' health. When Pacificare Health Systems, Inc., purchased FHP International, it paid $2.07 billion[17] for a company that had been valued at only $32 *million* when it converted to for-profit in 1985.[18] When U.S. Healthcare merged with Aetna Life & Casualty to form a huge HMO conglomerate, Healthcare's founder and chief executive officer, Leonard Abramson, gained a $1 *billion* bonus! The average health-care CEO earned $2.9 million in 1995. Several earned between $8.8 and $15.5 million per year,[19] and that doesn't take into account stock dividends paid to investors.

With so much money at stake, people need to think about euthanasia in the HMO context. They should be asked to imagine what it would be like knowing that the doctor who is licensed to kill them also benefits financially from doing it! They should consider how they would feel if an HMO doctor recommended assisted suicide for their spouse or child knowing that the doctor could lose money by referring them instead to prolonged specialized care that is far more expensive than euthanasia.

With HMOs becoming the norm, the built-in danger to patients should doctors ever be "licensed to kill" is likely to significantly mute euthanasia's current siren song—indeed, it may be the most effective argument against giving doctors a right to "assist" suicides in a culture that is losing its belief in an objective concept of right and wrong.

Protective guidelines do not work

When faced with these and other concerns, euthanasia advocates have a ready response: "We will have protective guidelines to prevent abuse."

An in-depth discussion about guidelines would prove that they do *not* protect. The experience of the Netherlands proves the point. Euthanasia is still *technically* illegal, but if "protective guidelines" are followed, doctors who kill patients are not prosecuted. These guidelines include:

- The request must be made entirely of the patient's own free will and not under pressure from others.
- The patient must have a lasting longing for death. In other words, the request must be made repeatedly over a period of time.
- The patient must be experiencing unbearable suffering.
- The patient must be given alternatives to euthanasia and time to consider these alternatives.
- There must be no reasonable alternatives to relieve suffering other than euthanasia.

- Doctors must consult with at least one colleague who has faced the question of euthanasia before.
- The patient's death cannot inflict unnecessary suffering on others.
- Only a doctor can euthanize a patient.
- The euthanasia must be reported to the coroner, with a case history and a statement that the guidelines have been followed.[20]

They may *sound* protective, but studies prove that the guidelines are completely ineffective. For example, a Dutch-sponsored study, generally known as the *Remmelink Report,* published statistics proving that physician-induced death accounts for nearly 9 percent of the 130,000 annual deaths in the Netherlands. According to these statistics, in 1990:

- 2,300 people died as the result of doctors killing them upon request (euthanasia).[21]
- 400 people died as a result of doctors providing them with the means to kill themselves (physician-assisted suicide).[22]

By making "rational suicide" a legally-recognized and enforceable right, the underlying message would be that all human lives are not of equal inherent worth.

- 1,040 people (an average of approximately 3 per day) died from involuntary euthanasia, meaning that doctors euthanized them without their knowledge or consent.[23] Of these, 14 percent were fully competent,[24] 72 percent had never given any indication that they would want their lives terminated,[25] and in 8 percent of the cases, doctors performed involuntary euthanasia despite the fact that they believed alternative options were still possible.[26] Moreover, in 45 percent of cases involving hospitalized patients who were involuntarily euthanized, the patients' families had no knowledge that their loved ones' lives were deliberately terminated by doctors.[27]
- Another 8,100 patients died as a result of doctors deliberately giving them overdoses of pain medication, not for the primary purpose of controlling pain, but with the specific intent to cause death.[28] In 61 percent of these cases (4,941 patients), the intentional overdose was given without the patient's consent.[29]

The above statistics indicate that Dutch physicians deliberately and intentionally ended the lives of 11,840 people by lethal overdoses or injections in one year. The figures also indicate that the *majority* of all doctor-induced deaths in the Netherlands are involuntary—so much for "protective guidelines"!

And these statistics are most likely *conservative:* Dutch guidelines *do* require doctors to report all euthanasia and assisted-suicide deaths to local prosecutors, but in the great number of cases—to avoid duplicate paperwork and the scrutiny of authorities—doctors deliberately falsify patients' death certificates, stating that the deaths are from natural causes.[30]

The *Remmelink Report* generated so much criticism that the Dutch conducted another study in 1995. Most of the statistics cited above were consistent with the new finding. However, the new study indicated that 55 percent of all physicians interviewed indicated they *had* "ended a patient's life without his or her explicit request" or that they "had never done so but that they could conceive of a situation in which they would." While more doctors reported their euthanasia activities than had in 1990, a whopping 59 percent of all Dutch doctors violate the guidelines by failing to comply with this "strict" requirement.[31] (This means, of course, that there is no true count of Dutch euthanasia-caused deaths.) Perhaps that is why the Dutch government is seriously considering weakening the reporting requirements!

Almost all pain can be effectively controlled.

Another reason why guidelines are irrelevant is that they are continually expanded over time. For example, in the 24 years that euthanasia has been a legitimate medical practice in the Netherlands, the guidelines have expanded to permit the killing of terminally-ill people, chronically-ill people, depressed people without organic diseases, and most recently babies born with birth defects based on "quality of life" considerations.[32]

Here in the United States, Jack Kevorkian has also stated that he operates using strict "guidelines." He and a small group of doctors have formed a group they call the "Physicians for Mercy" which published "protective guidelines" under which they claim to operate; requiring, for example, that people who wish to die because of a specified disease consult with a specialist in that condition prior to their life destruction, and that if pain is an issue, the person must be directed to a pain-control specialist. Yet, proving that guidelines are meant to be ignored, when Rebecca Badger wanted to kill herself because her purported multiple sclerosis (MS) pain was so severe, not only did Kevorkian *not* refer her to a pain specialist, there wasn't even a referral to a specialist who treats the neurological disease. Moreover, the autopsy showed that Badger did not have MS or any other determinable disease. Similarly, Kevorkian's guidelines promise that witnesses to his assisted killings will not have a financial interest in the person's demise. Yet the woman who accompanied Lisa Lansing to her February 1997 death in Michigan, widely believed to have been Kevorkian facilitated, was reportedly the sole beneficiary of Ms. Lansing's will, inheriting $500,000 from her dead friend.[33]

Protective guidelines give only the *appearance* of protection while offering no actual shelter from abuse. Worse, they act subversively to hide the truth about the victims of euthanasia. In short, guidelines serve no useful purpose other than to provide false assurances to the public. If that truth can be made to sink into the collective consciousness of the American public, the euthanasia movement should fade into obscurity.

Assisted suicide is a new form of oppression

At its core, all oppression is based on a division of human beings into different categories, some of whom receive special rights or greater protection than others because of a false belief that some humans are somehow better than other humans.

Oppression is especially insidious when formalized into law. The Jim

Crow statutes in the Old South, which legalized discrimination based on race, are illustrative. They not only gave African-Americans short legal shrift, but they actively promoted a racist and oppressive culture by giving the states' *imprimatur* to bigotry, thereby encouraging and legitimizing the overt, extra-legal racism then common in Southern society. Thus the very laws that required segregated schools were essential ingredients in creating the oppressive climate that permitted and even encouraged lynching, even though technically such vigilante murders were against the law.

So too would it be if the state created a legal right to "rational suicide." While the laws' wording would be couched in terms of compassion and liberty, language does not always mean what it *says* ("separate but equal" was *not* equal). By making "rational suicide" a legally-recognized and enforceable right, the underlying message would be that all human lives are not of equal inherent worth, that some of us (the healthy, able-bodied, and relatively happy) are worth protecting, even from self-destruction, while others of us (the "hopelessly ill") are people whose lives are of such little use that their deaths are best for all concerned. The impact of this legalized *healthism* would be no different from the consequences that flowed from institutionalizing racism in the law—it would create a new rationale for culling humans into privileged and oppressed classes, thereby influencing cultural outlook as well as impacting upon the state's legal obligations towards its citizens. The "right to die" would become a duty to die. In other words, "rational suicides" would not only be permitted but actively encouraged—just as the societal message behind Jim Crow laws promoted overt and covert racism.

Assisted suicide is unnecessary to alleviate suffering

It is not enough to be a naysayer about euthanasia; any in-depth discussion of assisted suicide must present positive alternatives. Happily, they exist in abundance.

First, unbeknownst to most people, almost all pain can be effectively controlled, including pain associated with arthritis, cancer, AIDS and multiple sclerosis. Indeed, regardless of the cause of pain, severity of condition, or type of disease, with proper medical treatment nearly every patient can have the pain eliminated or significantly reduced, adding tremendously to the quality of his or her life, and even its length.

The bad news is that doctors are notorious under-achievers when it comes to pain control. Many receive inadequate education in school and in continuing education about the subject. Doctors, like the lay public, also harbor excessive worries about addicting patients to drugs, or other side effects. Moreover, studies indicate that many doctors believe that only the severest pain requires treatment, thereby abandoning many chronic pain sufferers to their misery. Some doctors are insensitive to suffering, some do not take the time or effort to reevaluate their patients' pain on a regular and continuing basis, or indeed bother to *ask* their patients about their pain.[34] This being so, why should we trust doctors to kill us when many are doing a (generally) poor job of providing palliative relief?

Another point often overlooked in discussions about euthanasia is that dying people can remain "in control" by opting to die a peaceful and natural death with the assistance of hospice care. The goal of hospice is to provide whatever care patients need to enable them to die naturally (no efforts are made to prolong life), in peace, and with dignity. A typical hospice team includes a physician, nurses, social workers, psychological therapists and bereavement counselors, and volunteers. Since most hospice care occurs in the home (although there are hospice facilities), once a patient enters hospice, usually when the prognosis is life expectancy of 6 months or less, he or she can say good-bye to the impersonal hospitals and being "hooked up to machines" that so many of us fear during the dying process. Indeed, Dr. Carlos Gomez, a University of Virginia medical school professor and hospice doctor of international repute, says, "We now have it well within our technical means to alleviate, to palliate and comfort and control the worst symptoms of those of our fellow citizens who are terminally ill."[35]

How we decide the euthanasia controversy will determine the kind of society we live in.

The message of hospice is that each patient is valuable and important, that dying is an important stage of life that is worth living through and growing from—until death comes through natural processes. The euthanasia philosophy is just the opposite. By definition, euthanasia is a statement that life is *not* worth living, that the answer to dying, disability, or other "hopeless illness" is to artificially induce death and "get it over with." It is interesting to note a recent poll which showed that once people learned about the beneficence of hospice, support for legalizing assisted suicide fell some 20 points from the 70 percent range.[36]

Disabled people also have resources to help them lead interesting and productive lives, for example, there are independent living centers all around the country. Take Mark O'Brien, the Berkeley, California, journalist/poet who was the subject of an Oscar-winning documentary. Mark had polio at the age of six. He has been a complete quadriplegic for 42 years. The polio so profoundly disabled his musculature that Mark is dependent on an iron lung, rarely leaving the machine other than for a few hours a month when he is able to survive in a supine position on a ventilator, which allows him to be wheeled outside for an hour or so and to make personal appearances at lectures near his home. But almost his entire life is spent inside his yellow iron lung which dominates the small living room/kitchen of his one-bedroom loft apartment.

While Mark faces such considerable challenges, he enjoys life and lives it to the fullest—he is a published poet and journalist, and is writing his autobiography—in large part because of the independent-living movement: "Before I lived on my own," O'Brien told me, "I was afraid my life wouldn't amount to anything, that I couldn't do anything, that I would never be able to contribute to society. But because of independent living, I now have my own career, work at it, and live my own life. Because of independent living, I paid income taxes for the first time in my life last year. Most disabled people could achieve at least partial self-sufficiency with the appropriate services made available to them."[37]

The drive to legalize assisted suicide and euthanasia is the most important public-policy issue facing the country. In a very real sense, how we decide the euthanasia controversy will determine the kind of society we live in—and the one we will leave to our children. Seen in this light, the issue transcends what may or may not be good or bad, right or wrong, for individuals. It literally defines who and what we are as a society and a culture. That is why it is imperative that those of us who believe that legitimizing and legalizing the killing of the most weak and vulnerable among us would be an immoral, dangerous and oppressive policy should work overtime to create the kind of in-depth public dialogue that can and will defeat this pernicious social agenda. After all, our own lives may *depend* on victory.

Notes

1. *Compassion in Dying* v. *Washington,* 79 F.3d 790; *Quill* v. *Vacco,* 80 F.3d 716.

2. *Lee* v. *State of Oregon,* 891 F.Supp. 1421.

3. *Lee* v. *State of Oregon,* United States Court of Appeals for the Ninth Circuit, No 95-35804, official cite not yet available.

4. Toronto *Globe and Mail,* "The Slippery Slope That Leads to Death," by Andrew Coyne, November 21, 1994.

5. *The New Yorker,* "A Death of One's Own," by Andrew Solomon, May 22, 1995.

6. *Ladies' Home Journal,* "A Matter of Life or Death," January 1997.

7. Boston *Globe,* "Kevorkian Aid Ruled Homicide," (Reuters) September 4, 1996.

8. Board certified pain control specialist, Eric Chevlen, M.D., interview with author, September 6, 1996.

9. New York *Times,* "Beliefs" by Peter Steinfels, February 8, 1997.

10. *Compassion in Dying* v. *Washington,* supra.

11. *New England Journal of Medicine,* "Care of the Hopelessly Ill: Proposed Clinical Criteria for Physician-Assisted Suicide," by Timothy Quill, Vol. 327, November 3, 1992. See also Quill's book, *Death With Dignity: Making Choices and Taking Charge* (W.W. Norton and Co., New York, NY, 1993), in which he urges that assisted suicide be made available for nonterminally ill people.

12. New York *Times,* "Countdown to a Suicide," December 20, 1995.

13. *Suicide and Life Threatening Behavior,* "Empirically Based Criteria for Rational Suicide: A Survey of Psychotherapists," by James L. Werth, Jr., BS and Debra C. Cobia, Ed.D, Vol. 25(2), Summer 1995.

14. *Archives of Internal Medicine,* "Managed Care and Managed Death," by Daniel P. Sulmasy, O.F.M., M.D. Vol. 155, January 23, 1995, p. 134.

15. *USA Today,* "When Doctors Become Sub-Contractors of Medical Care," January 22, 1996.

16. Id.

17. *Wall Street Journal,* "Pacificare Health Agrees to Buy FHP International," by Rhonda L. Rundle, August 6, 1996.

18. Based on documents on file with the office of the California Attorney General.

19. New York *Times,* "Health Chief's Big Paychecks For Chopping Costs," by Milt Freudenheim, April 11, 1995.

20. *Regulating Death,* by Carlos F. Gomez, M.D. (Free Press, New York, NY, 1991).

21. *Medical Decisions About the End of Life,* "Vol. I: Report of the Committee to Study the Medical Practice Concerning Euthanasia." "Vol. II: The Study for the Committee on Medical Practice Concerning Euthanasia," The Hague, September 10, 1991. Known popularly as the *Remmelink Report.*

22. Id.

23. Id., p. 15.

24. *Remmelink Report,* Vol. II, p. 49, table 6.4.

25. Id., p. 50, table 6.6.

26. Id., table 6.5.

27. Id., table 6.8.

28. Id. at 58, table 7.2.

29. Id. at 72.

30. *L.Q. Review,* "The Law and Practice of Euthanasia in the Netherlands," by I.J. Keown, Vol. 108, pp. 67–68, note 16, 1992.

31. *New England Journal of Medicine,* 11/28/96.

32. For a detailed account of the degrading state of Dutch medical ethics, see *Seduced by Death,* by Herbert Hendin, M.D. (W.W. Norton & Co., New York, NY, 1996).

33. Detroit *Free Press,* "Officials Drop Suicide Probe," by Ariana E. Cha, February 12, 1997.

34. *Journal of Oncology Management,* "Lessons from the First Year of a State Cancer Pain Initiative," by Judith S. Blanchard and Debra D. Seale, November/December 1993.

35. Testimony of Carlos F. Gomez, M.D., before the U.S. House of Representatives Subcommittee on the Constitution, April 29, 1996.

36. Gallup Poll, sponsored by the National Hospice Organization, October 1994.

37. Mark O'Brien, interview with author, August 5, 1996.

Organizations to Contact

The editors have compiled the following list of organizations concerned with the issues debated in this book. The descriptions are derived from materials provided by the organizations themselves. All have publications or information available for interested readers. The list was compiled on the date of publication of the present volume; names, addresses, phone and fax numbers, and e-mail and Internet addresses may change. Be aware that many organizations take several weeks or longer to respond to inquiries, so allow as much time as possible.

American Foundation for Suicide Prevention (AFSP)
120 Wall St., 22nd Fl.
New York, NY 10005
(212) 363-3500
(800) 888-AFSP
fax: (212) 363-6237
e-mail: mtomecki@afsp.org
Internet: http://www.afsp.org

Formerly known as the American Suicide Foundation, the AFSP supports scientific research on depression and suicide, educates the public and professionals on the recognition and treatment of depressed and suicidal individuals, and provides support programs for those coping with the loss of a loved one to suicide. It opposes the legalization of physician-assisted suicide. The AFSP publishes a policy statement on physician-assisted suicide, the newsletter *Crisis*, and the quarterly *Lifesavers*.

American Life League (ALL)
PO Box 1350
Stafford, VA 22554
(703) 659-4171
fax: (703) 659-2586
e-mail: jbrown@all.org
Internet: http://www.all.org

ALL is a pro-life organization that provides information and educational materials to organizations opposed to physician-assisted suicide and abortion. Its publications include pamphlets, reports, the monthly newsletter *ALL About Issues*, and books such as *Choice in Matters of Life and Death* and *The Living Will*.

American Medical Association (AMA)
515 N. State St.
Chicago, IL 60610
(312) 464-4818
fax: (312) 464-4184
Internet: http://www.ama-assn.org

Founded in 1847, the AMA is the primary professional association of physicians in the United States. It disseminates information concerning medical breakthroughs, medical and health legislation, educational standards for physicians, and other issues concerning medicine and health care. It opposes physician-assisted suicide. The AMA operates a library and offers many publications, including its weekly journal, *JAMA*, the weekly newspaper *American Medical News*, and journals covering specific types of medical specialties.

American Society of Law, Medicine, and Ethics
765 Commonwealth Ave., Suite 1634
Boston, MA 02215
(617) 262-4990
fax: (617) 437-7596
e-mail: aslme@bu.edu
Internet: http://www.aslme.org

The society's members include physicians, attorneys, health care administrators, and others interested in the relationship between law, medicine, and ethics. The organization has an information clearinghouse and a library, and it acts as a forum for discussion of issues such as euthanasia and assisted suicide. It publishes the quarterlies *American Journal of Law and Medicine* and *Journal of Law, Medicine, and Ethics*, the newsletter *ASLME Briefings*, and books such as *Legal and Ethical Aspects of Treating Critically and Terminally Ill Patients*.

Center for Biomedical Ethics
3-110 Owre Hall
UMHC Box 33
Harvard St. and E. River Rd.
Minneapolis, MN 55455

The center studies the ethical implications of biomedical practices such as euthanasia, physician-assisted suicide, organ transplantation, and fetal tissue research. It publishes reading packets that provide introductory overviews to specific topics. Each packet includes a discussion of the topic's central issues, articles, a bibliography, additional reading materials, and a forecast of future debate on the topic. Packet titles include *Withholding or Withdrawing Artificial Nutrition and Hydration, Termination of Treatment of Adults*, and *Individual Responsibility for Health*. In addition, the center publishes articles, books, and reports.

Center for the Rights of the Terminally Ill
PO Box 54246
Hurst, TX 76054-2064
(817) 656-5143

The center opposes euthanasia and assisted suicide and works to protect the rights of the elderly, handicapped, sick, and dying. It believes legalized euthanasia would threaten these groups. The center provides educational materials and programs. Its publications include pamphlets such as *Living Wills: Unnecessary, Counterproductive, Dangerous* and *Can Cancer Pain Be Relieved?*

Choice in Dying
200 Varick St., 10th Fl.
New York, NY 10014-4810
(212) 366-5540
(800) 989-WILL
fax: (212) 366-5337
e-mail: cid@choices.org
Internet: http://www.choices.org

Choice in Dying educates medical professionals and the public about the legal, ethical, and psychological consequences of decisions concerning the terminally ill. For example, it provides physicians with information about the consequences of assisting in a patient's suicide or taking part in euthanasia. It publishes the quarterly newsletter *Choices* and the Question & Answer Series, which includes the titles *You and Your Choices, Advance Directives, Advance Directives and End-of-Life Decisions,* and *Dying at Home.*

Euthanasia Research and Guidance Organization (ERGO)
24829 Norris Ln.
Junction City, OR 97448-9559
phone and fax: (541) 998-1873
e-mail: ergo@efn.org
Internet: http://www.finalexit.org

ERGO advocates the passage of laws permitting physician-assisted suicide for the advanced terminally ill and the irreversibly ill who are suffering unbearably. It seeks to accomplish its goals by providing research data, addressing the public through the media, and helping raise campaign funds. The organization also provides the manual *Final Exit*, drug information, technique advice, and moral support to individuals contemplating suicide.

The Hastings Center
255 Elm Rd.
Briarcliff Manor, NY 10510
(914) 762-8500
fax: (914) 762-2124

Since its founding in 1969, the center has played a central role in responding to advances in medicine, the biological sciences, and the social sciences by raising ethical questions related to such advances. It conducts research and provides consultations on ethical issues. It does not take a position on issues such as euthanasia and assisted suicide but offers a forum for exploration and debate. The center publishes books, papers, guidelines, and the bimonthly *Hastings Center Report.*

The Hemlock Society
PO Box 101810
Denver, CO 80250
(303) 639-1202
(800) 247-7421
fax: (303) 639-1224
e-mail: hemlock@privatei.com
Internet: http://www.hemlock.org/hemlock

The society believes that terminally ill individuals have the right to commit suicide. It supports the practice of voluntary suicide and physician-assisted suicide for the terminally ill. The society publishes books on suicide, death, and dying, including *Final Exit*, a guide for those suffering with terminal illness and considering suicide. The society also publishes the *Hemlock Quarterly.*

Human Life International
7845 Airpark Rd., Suite E
Gaithersburg, MD 20879
(301) 670-7884
fax: (301) 869-7363

The pro-life Human Life International is a research, educational, and service organization. It opposes euthanasia, infant euthanasia, and assisted suicide. The group publishes books such as *Death Without Dignity*, pamphlets, and the monthly *HLI Reports*.

National Hospice Organization
1901 N. Moore St., Suite 901
Arlington, VA 22209
(703) 243-5900
(800) 658-8898
fax: (703) 525-5762
e-mail: drsnho@cais.com
Internet: http://www.nho.org

The organization works to educate the public about the benefits of hospice care for the terminally ill and their families. It seeks to promote the idea that with the proper care and pain medication, the terminally ill can live out their lives comfortably and in the company of their families. The organization opposes euthanasia and assisted suicide. It conducts educational and training programs for administrators and caregivers in numerous aspects of hospice care. It publishes the quarterlies *Hospice Journal* and *Hospice Magazine*, as well as books and monographs.

National Right to Life
419 Seventh St. NW, Suite 500
Washington, DC 20004-2293
(202) 626-8800
fax: (202) 737-9189

National Right to Life opposes euthanasia, physician-assisted suicide, and abortion because it believes these practices disregard the value of human life. The group organizes protests at the national and local level and publishes many articles, pamphlets, and reports to promote its position. Its *National Right to Life News* is published twice a month.

Park Ridge Center
211 E. Ontario, Suite 800
Chicago, IL 60611-3215
(312) 266-2222
fax: (312) 266-6068

The Park Ridge Center explores the relationship between health care, religious faith, and ethics. It facilitates discussion and debate about topics such as euthanasia and assisted suicide. The center publishes monographs, including *Active Euthanasia, Religion, and the Public Debate*, and the quarterly journal *Second Opinion*.

Bibliography

Books

Margaret P. Battin and Arthur G. Lipman, eds.   *Drug Use in Assisted Suicide and Euthanasia.* Binghamton, NY: Pharmaceutical Products Press, 1996.

Michael Betzold   *Appointment with Doctor Death.* Troy, MI: Momentum Books, 1993.

Donald W. Cox   *Hemlock's Cup: The Struggle for Death with Dignity.* Buffalo, NY: Prometheus Books, 1993.

Ronald M. Dworkin   *Life's Dominion: An Argument About Abortion, Euthanasia, and Individual Freedom.* New York: Knopf, 1993.

James M. Hoefler and Brian E. Kamoie   *Deathright: Culture, Medicine, Politics, and the Right to Die.* Boulder, CO: Westview Press, 1994.

Derek Humphry   *Final Exit: The Practicalities of Self-Deliverance and Assisted Suicide for the Dying.* Eugene, OR: Hemlock Society, 1991.

Stephen Jamison   *Final Acts of Love: Families, Friends, and Assisted Dying.* New York: Putnam, 1995.

Rita Marker   *Deadly Compassion: The Death of Ann Humphry and the Truth About Euthanasia.* New York: William Morrow, 1993.

Jonathan D. Moreno, ed.   *Arguing Euthanasia: The Controversy over Mercy Killing, Assisted Suicide, and the "Right to Die."* New York: Simon & Schuster, 1995.

G. Steven Neeley   *The Constitutional Right to Suicide: A Legal and Philosophical Examination.* New York: Peter Lang, 1994.

New York State Task Force on Life and the Law   *When Death Is Sought: Assisted Suicide and Euthanasia in the Medical Context.* New York: New York State Task Force on Life and the Law, 1994.

Sharhawk and Macha NightMare, eds.   *The Pagan Book of Living and Dying: Practical Rituals, Prayers, Blessings, and Meditations on Crossing Over.* New York: HarperCollins, 1998.

M. Scott Peck   *Denial of the Soul: Spiritual and Medical Perspectives on Euthanasia and Mortality.* New York: Harmony Books, 1997.

Timothy E. Quill   *Death and Dignity: Making Choices and Taking Charge.* New York: W.W. Norton, 1993.

Lonny Shavelson   *A Chosen Death: The Dying Confront Assisted Suicide.* New York: Simon & Schuster, 1995.

Joni Eareckson Tada   *When Is It Right to Die? Suicide, Euthanasia, Suffering, Mercy.* Grand Rapids, MI: Zondervan, 1992.

Robert F. Weir, ed.   *Physician-Assisted Suicide.* Bloomington: Indiana University Press, 1997.

Periodicals

Dennis Brodeur   "Ethical Issues and Legalizing Physician-Assisted Suicide," *Issues,* September/October 1996. Available from SSM Health Care System, 477 N. Lindbergh Blvd., St. Louis, MO 63141.

Dudley Clendinen   "When Death Is a Blessing and Life Is Not," *New York Times,* February 5, 1996.

Richard E. Coleson   "High Court Rejects Right to Assisted Suicide," *National Right to Life News,* July 9, 1997. Available from Suite 500, 419 Seventh St. NW, Washington, DC 20004.

Alan M. Dershowitz   "Pull the Plug on Dr. Death," *Los Angeles Times,* August 23, 1996. Available from Reprints, Times Mirror Square, Los Angeles, CA 90053.

Michael Fumento   "Drive By Evil," *National Right to Life News,* September 11, 1996.

Maggie Gallagher   "Shall Doctors Decide Who Lives or Dies?" *Human Events,* January 31, 1997. Available from 422 First St. SE, Washington, DC 20003.

Linda Ganzini and   "Psychiatry and Assisted Suicide in the United States,"
Melinda A. Lee   *New England Journal of Medicine,* June 19, 1997. Available from PO Box 9140, Waltham, MA 02254-9881.

Faye Girsh   "Supreme Court Unanimously Ambivalent," *Timelines,* July/August/September 1997. Available from The Hemlock Society USA, PO Box 101810, Denver, CO 80250.

Jane Gross   "New York Doctor at Center of Supreme Court Case on Assisted Suicide," *New York Times,* January 2, 1997.

Patrick D. Hopkins   "Why Does Removing Machines Count as 'Passive' Euthanasia?" *Hastings Center Report,* May/June 1997. Available from 255 Elm Rd., Briarcliff Manor, NY 10510.

Evan J. Kemp Jr.   "Could You Please Die Now?" *Washington Post National Weekly Edition,* January 13, 1997. Available from 1150 15th St. NW, Washington, DC 20071.

Douglas W. Kmiec   "There Is No Right to Kill," *Los Angeles Times,* March 8, 1996.

John Leo   "Good Sense on 'Right to Die,'" *U.S. News & World Report,* July 7, 1997.

Robert Lipsyte   "It's Life or Death: Who Can You Trust?" *New York Times,* January 12, 1997.

Los Angeles Times   "Assisted-Suicide Ruling: Door Flies Open on Intense Issue," March 8, 1996.

Ben Mattlin   "Walk a Mile in My Wheelchair," *Los Angeles Times,* April 12, 1996.

Eugene H. Methvin   "A Compassionate Killing," *Wall Street Journal*, January 20, 1997.

Terence Monmaney   "The Morality of Dying," *Los Angeles Times*, November 14, 1996.

New York Times   "Before the Court, the Sanctity of Life and of Death," January 5, 1997.

James P. Pinkerton   "When Law Overcomes Common Sense," *Los Angeles Times*, February 13, 1997.

Fazlur Rahman   "An Alternative to Kevorkian's Prescription," *Wall Street Journal*, November 2, 1995.

David G. Savage   "High Court Refuses to Grant Constitutional 'Right to Die,'" *Los Angeles Times*, June 27, 1997.

Lee R. Slome et al.   "Physician-Assisted Suicide and Patients with Human Immunodeficiency Virus Disease," *New England Journal of Medicine*, February 6, 1997.

Sheryl Stolberg   "Ending Life on Their Own Terms," *Los Angeles Times*, October 1, 1996.

Gary L. Thomas   "Deadly Compassion," *Christianity Today*, June 16, 1997.

David C. Thomasma   "When Physicians Choose to Participate in the Death of Their Patients: Ethics and Physician-Assisted Suicide," *Journal of Law, Medicine & Ethics*, vol. 24, no. 3, 1996.

U.S. Supreme Court   "Excerpts from Decision That Assisted Suicide Bans Are Constitutional," *New York Times*, June 27, 1997.

David Van Biema   "Death's Door Left Ajar," *Time*, July 7, 1997.

Index